*Advance Praise for*

"*Commended* is a remarkable Christian book that not only encourages believers to excel spiritually but does so with an unwavering commitment to the Gospel message. Its Gospel-centered approach is a refreshing and much-needed perspective in a world filled with self-help spirituality. Written by David Runge, this book is a beacon of hope and inspiration for those seeking to deepen their faith and walk with Christ. From the first chapter, the author's passion for Christ shines through. This book is infused with a profound understanding of the revolutionary power of commendation and takes the reader on a journey toward spiritual excellence that is rooted in the grace and truth of Jesus Christ. Through the pages of this book, you will discover that you are not just being encouraged—you are being transformed."

**Reverend Ronn Oren**
Senior Pastor, First Christian Church,
New Castle, Indiana

\*     \*     \*

"*Commended* is an oasis for the Christian reader who is spiritually thirsty and seeking to walk deeper with the Lord. It provides reassurances of God's love through the unique development of the many Bible characters and their stories. By the end of each chapter, I was drawn in more and more and wanted to keep reading. *Commended* presents God's love as both a unified and personalized entity, with each chapter's strengths and nuances bringing specific aspects of God's nature into fuller revelation. This book will not only strengthen believers who have been striving unnecessarily to please God through their own strength but also benefit Christians who seek to minister to others by bolstering their resources with new insights and winsome examples from the Bible."

**Rich Montgomery**, M.D.
Winston-Salem, North Carolina

\*     \*     \*

"David Runge is an encourager. When I first met him, I was going through a major life transition. David saw my pain and was one of the first to be a friend, a confidant, a shoulder to lean on, and a true brother in Christ. His friendship helped me stabilize, readjust, and get God's perspective on what I was going through.

When I discovered he was writing *Commended*, I knew it would be filled with all the great lessons David has learned that make his style of encouragement so effective. I couldn't wait to pick it up and have not been disappointed!

Relating engaging and creative dramatizations of Bible stories, David peers into what the biblical characters might have experienced as God commended them in their struggles. As I read, I was drawn to look deeper into my own life and into the Word. I was inspired, motivated, and challenged to know Jesus and feel his commendation for me even through tough times.

More than anything about the book, the blessings at the end of each chapter from David are so meaningful and special. Since I know him as a friend, it was as if each blessing were directed toward me for specific encouragement. Few books have had this kind of impact on me, and even if you don't know David, I venture to say that you will find the same to be true as well.

Don't miss reading David's book. I heartily commend it to you. Through it, you will learn to experience God's commendation at a whole new level."

**Brent H. Burdick**, D. Min.
Adjunct Professor of Missions, Gordon-Conwell Theological Seminary, Charlotte, North Carolina; Director, Lausanne Global Classroom; Author, *Gospel Issues for the Global Church*

\*　　\*　　\*

"When David Runge, my friend and brother, shared his book *Commended* with me, I had no idea the personal impact it would have on my life. From the very first chapter, I was captured by David's unique ability to weave a story around several Bible characters who received the commendation of Jesus. I found myself a part of each encounter with the Master. As an ambassador of encouragement, I have soaked this in, and in turn, I have learned more about and found fresh joy in my calling. I hope we receive more from this author's heart and pen."

**Reverend Jim Bevis**
President, CSR Ministries

\*　　\*　　\*

"*Commended* is a delight to read! David Runge presents rich biblical insights in a vivid writing style that helps us better understand those who encountered Jesus. Readers who seek greater security in God's commendation through the Gospel will find much encouragement here. Seasoned Christians will discover fresh insights in familiar accounts to help us know God better and love Him more."

**David Beaty**
Senior Pastor, River Oaks Community Church,
Clemmons, North Carolina

\*     \*     \*

"I find *Commended* to be a book everyone should read because we are all on a path to finding God's fulfillment in our lives. Through these pages, one will undoubtedly embark on a transformative journey that will bring rest to the soul on a quest for purpose as David exalts Jesus at the center of it all. *Commended* is a powerful resource radiating God's love in everyday experiences and encounters, and it instills the hope and faith one needs to carry on."

**Ben Banda**
Lead Pastor, Covenant Assembly, Lilongwe, Malawi

\*     \*     \*

"To know Jesus is to know God, and as Christians, we should desire to know God. So, we look to Christ as He fully reveals His Father. It is one thing to know the commands of Christ in Scripture, and this is important, as they teach us to honor our Savior. It is another thing to know the heart of Christ and to abide in the love He has for His own. In *Commended*, David Runge does a great job of revealing, through scripture, the heart of our Lord toward us, enabling us to rest in His pleasure as we live out our design."

**Carey Edgren**
Senior Pastor, Terrace Lake Church, Columbus, Indiana

\*     \*     \*

"Every one of us faces the struggle of what path to choose, which David Runge addresses in this excellent work. As Jesus mentions in Matthew 7:13-14, we have a choice to make: either follow the lesser-used narrow path that leads to life or the much wider, pleasant, self-pleasing, nice-looking but deceitful one that leads to death.

Now, that might sound like a big life-and-death decision, and it is. But it also applies to our day-to-day life, the common things that might not seem so important, like we find in the story of Martha and Mary in Luke 10:38-42. Martha was working hard to prepare to receive her guests. Mary was supposed to help but chose to sit at Jesus's feet instead. The question, of course, is who has made the right choice?

David brings the answer to this question down to earth. He talks about his own experiences and those of many others. He reflects on our aspirations in life, the choice between the work, the success, the stability, or the relationship and the peace and the joy. He explores the assault of external factors like religion and life's struggles and the internal factor of our natural disposition. And he rests in the joy of Jesus's approval as he pursues the goal of bringing Jesus pleasure."

**Reverend Storly Michel**
Station Director Radio-TV 4VEH,
"The Evangelistic Voice of Haiti"

\*　　\*　　\*

"The book you are about to read is not the product of a few weeks or months of research. Its contents have resulted from precious time of fellowship with the Lord—seeking His face in prayer. It's a great honor and joy to recommend this book. It will inspire you, challenge you, and increase your hunger for fellowship with the Lord. As you study and read this book, may the Holy Spirit touch you so deeply that you will enter into a new place of fellowship with our Lord Jesus Christ.

I encourage you to pray and seek the face of the Lord as you proceed. This is an excellent book—enjoyable to read and easy to follow. May you enjoy His Presence and His peace in ever-increasing measure through the pages of this book as brother David Runge reveals the heart of God for you. And may your heart be opened to His love as a result, drawing you to discover Him deeper in His Word.

*Commended* reveals the truth about the love of our Father God. He loves us so much with His great and everlasting love. He has a great plan for every person on the face of the Earth. He loves all people and is proud of us as His dear children.

David Runge reveals the answer to our deepest need. Please read this with an open heart. May the Lord bless you as you read. *Commended* is the book you have been looking for, and to have this book in your hands—it's an answer to your prayers.

I have known Brother David for over twelve years now. He is a man of integrity and has a passion to lead others into deep fellowship with the Lord. I encourage you to read *Commended* with the Bible open—because the Bible is the only infallible word of God."

**Reverend Stephen B. Banda**
President, Apostolic Church of Pentecost, Malawi, Africa

\*　　\*　　\*

"In *Commended*, author David Runge has written not only an interesting and inspiring book but also an important book. Important because since the fall of mankind, our species has entered life without an innate clear-cut direction, a well-defined purpose, and a comprehension of the source of its fulfillment. Even newly hatched sea turtles can make their way to the surf within minutes.

The book draws on the author's experience, not only as a counselor and pastor, but also as a corporate pilot. He understands that well before takeoff, he must have a flight plan with all the fixes and waypoints leading to the destination airport. He must have a weather briefing and familiarity with every possible impediment to a safe and pleasant flight.

After reading *Commended*, it occurred to me that all these prerequisites for flight have parallels that can be applied to discovering how best to invest our brief time here on Earth.

Practically every page illuminates the secrets to a meaningful life with purpose, joy, and satisfaction. According to David, in declaring that He is the way, the truth, and the life, Jesus, somewhat mystically, reveals that seeking and receiving God's commendation is the flight plan for fulfillment and joy toward our ultimate destination of eternal life. Yet we often veer off course because we try to follow the mistaken path of performance.

Before I read *Commended*, many of the passages of Scripture that I had cobbled together to form my approach to living were merely biblical devices. That changed when the author revealed them in the new light of grace, igniting my joy in God's approval, affirmation, and pleasure."

**Kent Weathersby**
Captain (Ret.), United Airlines

\*     \*     \*

"*Commended* is a fascinating and captivating book written by David Runge. In it, he looks at the risen Lord Jesus Christ through the lens of how he has experienced Him and how Jesus revealed Himself to him. In this book, the author showcases the deep passion of his heart through several biblical characters who received the commendation of Jesus. From the very first chapter till the end, the author's passion for Jesus and for a personal relationship with Him is evident.

This book establishes that even in the very worst, most challenging days of our lives, we can find joy and happiness through God's approval and affirmation. It brings out fresh perspectives through inspiring narratives of people who received the joy of Jesus Christ through acts of faith, hope, and love.

*Commended* provides hope, assurance, and affirmation for those who seek an intimate relationship with Jesus, which will change their perspective on life. Reading this book will result in fresh insights and a deeper understanding of God revealed in the day-to-day life so that when we meet our Lord Jesus, we can receive His commendation. 'Well done, good and faithful servant.'"

**Reverend Dr. S. Duraiswamy**
Director Partner Relations, Evangelical Church of India

\*       \*       \*

"In *Commended*, the author not only takes us on his personal faith journey but gives us a realistic, down-to-earth look at the journeys and struggles of several biblical characters, both well-known and lesser known. As David so aptly shows us, we do best in our journey to and with our God when we concentrate on pleasing Him, not just by what we do (our obedience and service to Him), but also by seeking to please Him by our faith, our hope, and our love, no matter what situations we face in life or what circumstances we may encounter in our daily walk with

Him. As you take in the rich stories from the scriptures and from the author's own life, you will grow in your understanding of relationship with God and what actually pleases Him. Our goal as Christians is to bring joy to our Father by our lives, just as Jesus did. As the Hebrew writer put it:

'Therefore, since we are surrounded by so great a cloud of witnesses, let us also lay aside every weight, and sin which clings so closely, and let us run with endurance the race that is set before us, looking to Jesus, the founder and perfecter of our faith, who for the joy that was set before Him endured the cross, despising the shame, and is seated at the right hand of the throne of God.' (Heb. 12:1-3 ESV)

This book is a great volume for personal or small group study and could easily be incorporated into a Bible class format. I have known the author for many years and am happy to heartily recommend this book."

**Don Collins**, M.D.
Piqua, Ohio

\*      \*      \*

"When I read a book that communicates grace, I feel a weight lifted from my heart and, at the same time, a call and strength to pursue God more passionately. *Commended* does that."

**Jeannette S**.
Hope, Indiana

\*      \*      \*

"*Commended* makes my heart sing!"

**Myra F.**
Columbus, Indiana

# Commended

Finding Your Joy in God's
Approval, Affirmation, and Pleasure
(EVEN ON YOUR WORST DAYS)

# David Runge

Foreword by Alan Wright

Ballast Books, LLC
www.ballastbooks.com

Copyright © 2024 by David Runge

Unless otherwise noted, scripture quotations are from the ESV® Bible
(The Holy Bible, English Standard Version®), copyright © 2001 by
Crossway Bibles, a publishing ministry of Good News Publishers.
Used by permission. All rights reserved. Scripture quotations marked
"NLT" are taken from the New Living Translation, copyright © 1996,
2004, 2015 by Tyndale House Foundation. Used by permission
of Tyndale House Publishers, Inc., Carol Stream, Illinois 60188.
All rights reserved.

ISBN: 978-1-962202-08-4

Printed in the United States of America

Published by Ballast Books
www.ballastbooks.com

For more information, bulk orders, appearances, or speaking requests,
please email: info@ballastbooks.com

*To Kathy, my bride and joy.*

*And to all those who seek the joy of God's affirmation and pleasure.*

*In your presence there is fullness of joy; at your right hand are pleasures for evermore.*

—Psalm 16:11b

# Author's Note

This is not a how-to book. It does not offer ten easy steps to pleasing God. Neither is it an academic theological study. It is a look at Jesus through the eyes of those who encountered Him as He revealed Himself uniquely to each one.

God loves to reveal Himself to those who seek Him. He will reveal Himself as we journey together through this book. But He will also reveal Himself beyond the words on these pages. He will speak into our hearts. He will reveal aspects of Himself that we most need to hear. His words will bring new life. Most of all, He will speak of His pleasure in us as His beloved.

When He speaks correction, His words will bring no shame, only relief and joy. Words of relief because He already knows everything about us and we no longer need to hide. He knows our worst but sees and calls out our best. We can cease our striving for His approval. Words of joy because even unmasked, we will experience His grace and love. So write down what you are hearing. His words are precious. You don't want to lose them!

# Contents

## LOVE

## THE PRIZE

"My Lord God, I have no idea where I am going. I do not see the road ahead of me. I cannot know for certain where it will end. Nor do I really know myself, and the fact that I think that I am following Your Will does not mean that I am actually doing so. But I believe that the desire to please You does in fact please You. And I hope I have that desire in all that I am doing."

— Thomas Merton

# *Foreword*

When our little boy, Bennett, got sick for the first time, it broke my heart. At first, we thought the toddler was just being fussy. But when we took him to the pediatrician, we learned that the little fellow had a raging ear infection.

The doctor prescribed an oral antibiotic that we were to administer with a medicine dropper. Little Bennett so despised the drug that he wouldn't swallow it. The earache raged on as the tot refused the antidote.

Desperate and worried, we called the pediatrician and asked what to do. What he told us was disturbing—we'd have to hold the boy down, pinch his nose, and force him to swallow the ill-tasting concoction.

Ugh. I'll never forget the awful moment. I pinned our beloved firstborn to the kitchen floor and held his nose while my sweet wife fought back tears and squirted the medicine into his mouth.

After Bennett swallowed the disdained liquid, he cried, looked straight at us, and said, "Do you think that made God happy?"

We moved from choking back tears to fighting back giggles.

He was only three or four years old, but I suppose he had already discerned the most important question in our family!

*Do you think that made God happy?*

I've never forgotten little Bennett's query because, in the end, it is the most important question.

It's the question my friend David Runge addresses profoundly in these pages—and the answers he brings are sweet to the soul.

*What makes God happy? What does God commend?* As Runge shows us, we get the answer most clearly in Christ, the God-man, Who revealed to us the Father. Jesus's life lets us peer into the pleasures of God—into all that God commends.

These pages are worth our attention because they bring fresh bread for the soul—and it all seems hot from the oven of an author's heart. The aroma is enticing. These pages also are deserving of our time because David Runge has found fresh ways to tell old stories to unleash new hope.

But by far the central reason these pages warrant our focus and enjoyment is that they bring us close to the heart of God. To discover what God commends is to discover His heart—His deepest nature.

So, get ready to discover God's heart—get ready to be surprised.

Someone has said, "Wouldn't it be a shame to spend your life baking apple pies for God only to find out that He doesn't like apple pie?"

Most well-meaning Christians think our efforts at righteousness make God happy. We want to prove ourselves to God. We struggle with unmerited favor. I suppose we gravitate to law because grace feels so foreign, so preposterous.

Prepare to be surprised by the preposterous grace of God that spills forth from this author's pen. Allow yourself to drink in blessing.

Get ready to be commended by God.

I wholeheartedly *commend* all that follows.

**Alan Wright**
Sr. Pastor, Reynolda Church
National Radio communicator
Author of seven books, including *The Power to Bless* and *Seeing as Jesus Sees*

# *Preface*

## Our Joy in His Pleasure

What if much of what we believe about pleasing God is remarkably wrong? Would that cause you to question? To reevaluate? To ponder? What if it were much simpler than we thought? What if we could experience ongoing joy in the assurance of God's affirmation, approval, and pleasure, even on our worst days? And why is this experience of joy so important? Exploring answers to these questions will make all the difference as we pursue God.

Like a GPS warning "recalculating" prompts us to reconsider our current route, certain events trigger our need to evaluate life. Marriage, divorce, birth, death, promotion, job loss, midlife crisis, and other unexpected intrusions may prompt big questions such as: Why am I here? What is my purpose? Is there a God? And if so, what does it take to please Him, and why would it matter? For me, an unplanned retirement at sixty-seven years of age in August of 2021 spurred such a reflection.

Admittedly, life's road behind me is much longer than that which lies in front. I had settled the question "Is there a God?" in 1971 as a senior in high school when I discovered Him in a new light. The joy of this discovery—of a personal God who loves, forgives, and takes great pleasure in me—was palpable. It was a joy that would define and impact the rest of my life. Yet I soon discovered this joy was under constant attack on multiple fronts.

## Assaults on Joy

We all face trials as broken people living in a broken world. I experienced distress resulting from two Ds in chemistry my freshman year in college, quashing my plans for veterinary school—I eventually graduated in three years and went on to graduate school in counseling. Then there was the vulnerability of falling in love with a girl who was not yet in love with me—in short time she said yes, and is still saying yes, forty-eight years later. Not to mention the weight of career changes from marriage and family counselor to business jet pilot, missionary, pastor, and back to pilot, and job losses (at least one of which was partially self-inflicted) that assailed my joy. But all of these setbacks were temporary, with joy returning even before the storms passed.

The most insidious assault on my joy, however, has been religion. Or more accurately, religiosity. It is a counterfeit religion devoid of relationship. It is the pull of performance, demands of dos and don'ts, and the appeal of appearances, taking what God intends to be a faith that frees and corrupting it into a religion that restrains. It is constant, yet subtle. It results in an affected piety and zeal designed to impress man, but it nauseates God. It distorts the reality of what pleases God and results in His pleasure and affirmation, making His approval and commendation seem impossible. And because it seems impossible, we pursue religious activity and the approval of man that never satisfies as an attempt to bolster our identity, sense of meaning, and happiness. As a person of faith, it is my desire to live a life pleasing to God, one that He commends, to experience joy in my relationship with Him, but how do I get this right?

I have seen many people from all walks of life, all over the world, even those who have known God for many years, get it wrong. I include myself. Although my church experience has been consistently grace-oriented over the years, I am often ensnared by the lure of religious performance. Some days bring regret about what I have left undone, remorse at a distasteful thought or action, or arrogant pride in some accomplishment, insight, or act of service. I imagine God's disappointment at my failings, or His approval at my attempts at self-justification. How do I take pleasure in my relationship with Him on such days? I must be clear on what actually pleases Him and what brings Him joy. It is the only way to resist the seduction of a religious spirit. It is a spirit Jesus confronted regularly in His encounters with the Pharisees of His time. It is still active today.

## The Great Need

This begs the question: why do I want to write this book? To paraphrase the words of C.J. Mahaney, author of *Humility: True Greatness*, anyone who would presume to write on pleasing God should be immediately considered suspect.[a] I am no exception. I am not there. This is a journey of discovery. I have written this as much for myself as for you. It is based on a sermon series I shared in 2014. It forced me back to the basics, and over time, my discovery of what actually pleases God and brings Him joy has weakened the influence of the religious spirit and rekindled the joy of my first encounters with Christ.

---

[a] C. J. Mahaney writes, "If I met someone presuming to have something to say about humility, automatically I'd think him unqualified to speak on the subject." Mahaney, C.J. (2005). Humility: True Greatness, Introduction, Colorado Springs: Multnomah Books.

Resisting the religious spirit and walking in the consistency of the joy of the Father's approval, affirmation, and pleasure becomes even more important as the assaults on our joy increase. Some troubling signs reveal a great need. Researchers point to recent declines in happiness, mental health, and an increase in anxiety and depression, especially among Gen Z.[b]

What are we to make of these revelations? Certainly, the isolation caused by the COVID-19 pandemic is a significant factor and emphasizes the importance of relationships. However, meaningful relationships and the joy they bring have been in decline for several decades. Harvard professor and researcher Arthur Brooks explains, "I believe the happiness crisis in America is at its core a crisis of our personal and shared sense of meaning. The institutions of meaning have all weakened dramatically in the past two decades."[1]

Brooks goes on to describe four institutions of meaning: faith, family, friendship, and work. He notes religious affiliation and practice have dropped significantly, marriage rates have fallen by 38 percent since 2000, and the percentage of people with fewer than three close friends has doubled since 1990.[2] Don't miss the fact that the drop in religious affiliation and practice implies a decline in relationships, even among people of faith, and a decline in personal relationships with God. This is critical. It is possible to have an accurate theological knowledge of God's love, care, and provision, which will bring a measure

---

[b] An Associated Press article from May 2020 reports only 14 percent of American adults say they are very happy, down from 31 percent in 2018. This figure had never been below 29 percent since data collection began in 1972 (June 16, 2020, by Associated Press). Psychiatrist.com reports 42 percent of Gen Z have been diagnosed with a mental health condition, with anxiety and depression topping the list, good or excellent mental health, up to 75 percent, while Gen Z is the least likely generation to report good or excellent mental health at only 45 percent affirming (November 9, 2022, by Staff Writer, Psychiatrist.com).

of security, peace, and joy in life's trials. But deeper, consistent joy is born in affirming relationships. Knowing we are valued and approved, warts and all, is essential in forming our sense of identity and purpose. The religious spirit cannot provide this. It does not affirm. It demands we work harder, hide our faults, and put on a false front. It is a fraud.

## The Great Answer

What if pursuing God's affirmation and approval is the answer to finding our purpose, joy, and happiness? What if experiencing His joy and pleasure could strengthen the weakened institutions of meaning impacting our lives and demolish the draw of the religious spirit?

Our motivation for this pursuit is the key to its success and reward. Do we seek to justify ourselves, to earn God's approval? This approach leads only to more desperation, instability, and pain. However, if we seek to bring joy to the One who loved us first, our relationship with Him deepens, and we are on the proper path. As we look for road signs to guide the way as we travel, we want to recognize what brings God joy, receives His commendation, and merits His approval. It's probably not what you think.

What drew you to this book? Do you long to receive a commendation from Jesus?

Perhaps you are well aware of His love for you, of the joy He takes in your fellowship with Him, and you long to bring Him greater joy. I invite you to discover what He values.

Maybe you have tasted joy in your relationship with Him but have been lured away by a performance-based religion and long to rediscover that which you first knew. I invite you to be freed from external expectations and find joy in His heart for you as you return to your first love.

Perhaps you feel you could never please Him. You may have grown up in a religious environment focusing on what to believe, how to act, and what to say, and never discovered the joy of a personal relationship with God. I invite you to discover His longing for you and experience the joy of His affirmation and love as He reveals Himself on our journey together.

Maybe you believe your life is extraordinarily normal with no great accomplishments to offer Him. I invite you to discover the simplicity of pleasing God.

Possibly you have never heard the words "I'm proud of you" from a parent or spouse and feel you could never do enough to please, assuming God shares this disappointment. I invite you to hear His word: "You are my beloved child, in whom I am well pleased."

Perhaps faults and failures assail you and you believe all is lost, you are too far gone, and God could never love you. I invite you to discover that Jesus's greatest affection is meant for you.

Maybe you have heard of Jesus and wonder what it takes to please Him, to be accepted by Him. I invite you to discover that He is pleased with your curiosity, and to have it satisfied.

Or could it be that you have distanced yourself from God, assuming you must toe the line and follow rigid rules to gain His approval? You might believe He is angry at you. If so, I hope you will stay with me, because you have been fed a religious lie. As pastor and author Alan Wright observes in his book *The Power to Bless*, "Religion says, 'I messed up. My father is going to be so mad.' The Gospel says, 'I messed up; better call Dad.'"[3]

I have good news for you. God loves you. You are worth everything to Him. I pray you will discover this truth as we continue. But know this—your desire to explore how to please God originated from Him and already pleases Him!

I invite you to join me on this quest. We will address the human need we all share for relationships and commendation. However, we will put people's approval in its rightful place, elevating the fundamental significance of receiving approval from God.

The Bible teaches much about what God desires of those who follow Jesus, and many excellent books have been written on the subject. They are worthy of our attention. Our journey will be different. The Bible also reveals stories of those who caused Jesus to marvel, comment, and commend—those who touched His heart and brought Him joy. These will be our focus.

In most cases, those whom Jesus commended are not the great names of the Bible and have no great accomplishments to claim. They are often mentioned only once and then disappear from the biblical narrative. But they each discovered something unique about Jesus as He revealed Himself. Something that caused them to respond in a way that elicited His response and approval. These are folks I identify with, and we will look at Jesus through their eyes, as understanding the expression of their hearts changes everything about our view of God and how we approach Him. Would you like to know their secret? You will receive hope that pleasing God is actually possible. You will discover how God really feels about you—it is good news! You will feel the weight of performance-based religion lifting from your heart. Your passion to pursue God and enjoy His company will reignite. You will gain a clearer, greater view of Jesus. And you will discover joy in Jesus's affirmation, His approval, and His pleasure in you. Join me as we begin.

To start, we need to explore the importance of commendation. We do so because our deepest human need is to be valued, affirmed, and loved. We all need approval. It is part of the divine design. It is essential to our mental, physical, and spiritual health. And its absence is catastrophic. A pardoned felon, in more ways than one, leads us as we begin. His story is revealed in our first chapter.

# Section 1

⋯⋅✦◆✦⋅⋯

# The Quest

# Chapter 1

# The Power of Commendation

*The biggest obstacle on my journey of trust has been an
oppressive sense of insecurity, inadequacy, inferiority, and
low self-esteem. I have no memory of being held, hugged,
or kissed by my mother as a little boy.*

—Brennan Manning[4]

On March 1, 2018, David Bacon sat glued to his television. He was fifty-five years old, or twenty-five years old, or two years old, depending on how you counted. Chronologically, he was a senior citizen; however, his new birth occurred in 1993 when he gave his life to Christ. And now, freed from prison two years earlier, he leaned forward on his sofa, blinking to clear the teary mist as he strained for a clearer view of the image on the screen.

He recognized the Reverend Billy Graham's casket. How could he forget? His hands had helped construct the modest pine coffin in 2006, twelve years earlier in a prison workshop in Angola, where he had been serving a life sentence for murder. His throat tightened with a mixture of pride and gratitude at the great honor and privilege of his gift to the man. Reverend Graham had led him to freedom and new life and was now free of his earthly form, risen to eternal life with Christ. David shared with two reporters the story of his connection with Billy Graham, noting his humility, his love, and his simple message of the redemption in Christ available to anyone.

David Bacon, awarded clemency in December 2016, told his story of freedom from not only his spiritual prison but as a man freed from the prison walls of Angola. Listen to his words as he recounts the formation of his early life in the *Charlotte Observer.* "This comes from hindsight: I was looking for love, guidance, acceptance, approval," Bacon said. "When you're young, you'll do anything to get it. I couldn't get that from my father."[5]

Hear the power of affirmation evident in David's transformation and freedom as a Christ follower as imparted to the *Baptist Message.* "While incarcerated, with help from ministries like Billy Graham's, I got to know God, and developed a relationship with God, and received Jesus as Lord and found love, guidance, acceptance, and approval that I didn't find with my biological father, my earthly father," Bacon said. "I found it with THE Father."[6]

Commendation is critical to our identity and sense of self-worth. Consider again the words of David Bacon. Catch the longing as he describes his search for love, acceptance, guidance, and approval, along with the pain of its absence. Hear the desperate willingness to do anything to find it. Perhaps you can identify. If so, you are not alone. We all enjoy an "attaboy." Affirming commendation is necessary for one's healthy development. We can't write it off. David Bacon's story reveals the devastating effects of its lack. What did David discover about God that changed everything? He received the joy of the Father's affirmation and commendation. He found a new, true, and secure identity in the Father's approval.

## Wired for Relationship

"Wilson! Wilson!" Chuck Noland's anguished voice cries out as his companion, washed overboard, unnoticed from their crude makeshift raft, drifts lifelessly away. "I'm sorry, Wilson. I'm sorry," Chuck sobs as he abandons his friend's rescue, struggling back to their raft where they had escaped an uninhabited island after a FedEx crash four years earlier. Of course, Wilson is only a volleyball, personified by Chuck Noland, Tom Hanks' character in *Cast Away*.[7] Chuck's desperate attempt to cope with his stranded isolation led to Wilson's conception and provoked the agony of his loss.

What makes Chuck's heartache at abandoning Wilson so intense? We are wired to be in relationships. In their absence, we will do anything to fabricate them. Because we are designed for relationships, the affirmation we receive in relationships is critical to our development and sense of self. Our identity never forms in isolation. Commendation helps shape our identity as a potter's hands shape clay into an artist's desired form. Others observe and validate our gifts, notice what is important to us, and affirm what they see in us. So why does our search for affirmation often leave us empty, unfulfilled, and feeling there must be something more?

## A Fickle Friendship

Like most teenagers, I wanted to be cool. But face it, some, like the "Fonz" of *Happy Days* fame, have it. Others, like me, don't. So I hung out mostly with band kids and the German Club. That is until my junior year. I was seated next to one of the cool guys in chemistry class. You know, the multisport jock type. We had an unverbalized agreement. He befriended me, and I let him glance at my paper during exams. At the end of the semester, our teacher called us up one by one to tell us what our grades would be. My turn arrived. "David, I know what you have been doing on the exams," the teacher said. "I'm giving you a C. You were one point from getting a D, and if you hadn't gotten that point, I would have given you the D."

Apparently, I was not as clever, or as good a chemistry student, as I thought. I don't know what grade my buddy got, but we didn't hang out much after that class. The source of my affirmation changed in my senior year. But more on that later.

Like the popular high school kid who seems to be your best friend one day and shuns you the next, the affirmation of others is often fickle, even performance based. In the case of the self-esteem movement, it is often not even related to actual accomplishments. We may receive accolades from others, but like a drug that promises more than it delivers and enslaves us to its demands, we continue to seek the next fix, receiving ever-diminishing returns. What are we to do? If affirmation is so important to our sense of worth, the development of our identities, and our enjoyment of relationships, how do we get there?

## The Something More

C.S. Lewis, Oxford professor, author, and lay theologian writes, "If I find in myself a desire which no experience in this world can satisfy, the most probable explanation is that I was made for another world."[8] This applies to our search for affirmation. If we find in ourselves a need for affirmation that no earthly relationship can satisfy, the most probable explanation is we are made for a deeper relationship, one not of this world. To say we are wired or designed for relationships implies a designer, a creator, God, and He has provided a roadmap.

Our starting point, our on-ramp, if you will, is to reject the lie that He is disappointed in us or angry with us. We come to understand He has created us for the purpose of His pleasure as we exist in relationship with Him. This takes the focus off of us and puts it where it belongs. We arrive at our destination when we learn to receive affirmation from God, an affirmation unchangeable, not dependent on our performance, which speaks to our hearts that we are His beloved children and of great worth to Him. God's affirmation is rooted in an unalterable love, creating in us a desire to love and please Him in return. Now that we have examined our need for approval, we will explore the significance of finding the proper source. Because finding the right source is the game changer.

Much of Genesis, the first book of the Bible, is devoted to Jacob, a man destined for greatness. Although, as second-born after his brother Esau, he had no rightful claim to leadership. Let's look at his journey in our next chapter as he progresses from deceiver, to believer, to receiver. Jacob discovers the source of commendation elevating him to great significance, finding joy and a new, true, and secure identity in God's affirmation and approval. Receive a blessing to apprehend what comes next.

*See what kind of love the Father has given to us, that we should be called children of God; and so we are.*

—1 John 3:1a

I bless you, beloved child of God,
With release from your struggle for acceptance.
May you discover the joy,
Of unconditional love and affirmation.
May you receive the blessing and commendation,
Of your Heavenly Father,
And find your joy,
In His approval, affirmation, and pleasure.

# Chapter 2

## Consider the Source

*Your fulfillment in life depends on your relationship with Father. The depth of your soul and personal maturity depends on your intimacy with Father.*

—Fred Hartley III[9]

### Deceiver: A Counterfeit Identity

Sweat drenched Jacob's brow, dripped down his neck, and soaked his borrowed garments, although it was not hot, nor was he exerting himself as he approached the tent belonging to his father, Isaac. The ruse he was about to perpetrate caused his distress. He carried his father's favorite meal, prepared by his mother, Rebekah, into Isaac's chamber. This had not been his idea, but his mother had insisted. "Quick, bring me two young goats from the herd," Rebekah had said. "I heard your father send your brother, Esau, to hunt for fresh game so that he could eat it and then bless him. I'll send you with the stew I make, and you can receive your father's blessing instead."

9

Jacob resisted at first but remembered his brother selling him his birthright years earlier for a pot of stew. Rebekah had tied goat skin to Jacob's hands and neck to simulate Esau's ruddy feel and dressed him in his brother's clothes. Jacob warmed to the plan. Now his neck and hands itched. The stew's aroma, mixed with the smell of his brother's sweat-stained clothes, had its desired effect. Though Isaac's vision failed, his sense of smell and touch remained strong. He embraced Jacob, felt his hands and neck, and pronounced the blessing that belonged to Esau.

"See, the smell of my son
is as the smell of a field that the Lord has blessed!
May God give you of the dew of heaven
and of the fatness of the earth
and plenty of grain and wine.
Let peoples serve you,
and nations bow down to you.
Be lord over your brothers,
and may your mother's sons bow down to you.
Cursed be everyone who curses you,
and blessed be everyone who blesses you!"
—Genesis 27:27b–29

Jacob backed away and exited the tent. But the satisfaction of a successful deception left him empty, as one who has tasted a sweet pastry but is unable to swallow. What was the result of this deception? Jacob may have received a blessing, a commendation, but he lost his relationship with his father as well as his brother Esau. He would have some bad days, experiencing much pain, before these relationships would be restored.

Let's follow Jacob's story as he learns to receive his Heavenly Father's blessing.

## Believer: The Birth of Identity

*Will it make any difference?* Jacob prepared to face his brother, Esau. Years later, Jacob still remembered the day he had fled to the home of his uncle Laban. Esau had vowed to kill Jacob for stealing his blessing, and Jacob had left town quickly. He had escaped Esau's wrath but not the deception and conflict that clung to him as dung clings to sandals. He would be defrauded as well in the very place he had run for refuge.

The deception Laban had perpetrated still stung. Laban had caused Jacob to work for him twice as long for his daughter Rachel's hand in marriage. He had then attempted to cheat Jacob out of his agreed-upon share of the goat flock. Jacob's God-inspired breeding strategy had foiled that plan, and Laban was not happy. He pursued the fleeing Jacob, resulting in a bloodless encounter only after Laban received a warning from God.[c]

Certainly, God had been with Jacob the whole time, he reflected. He had believed in God but was yet to experience what God had purposed for him. God had appeared to Jacob in a dream, blessing him at Bethel, and Jacob promised himself there to God. He had even sent angels to meet with Jacob in anticipation of his encounter with Esau. However, last night was different. God had appeared to him in person, and Jacob grabbed Him and would not let go, demanding a blessing. The wrestling match had persisted all night, until God blessed Jacob and have him a new name, Israel. Jacob had prevailed. But his

---

[c] The full story of Jacob's life and his role in the formation of Israel is extensive, comprising nearly half the book of Genesis from chapters twenty-five through fifty.

resulting limp revealed the struggle's cost as God had put his hip out of joint.

And now, as Jacob prepared to meet Esau, his confidence increased. He was sure. What had happened the previous night would make a difference. Though he had sent servants ahead with much livestock as an appeasement, he now went on ahead of his servants; his wives, Leah and Rachel; and all of their children to face his brother at the fore.

Esau's approach was daunting. Jacob's eyes widened and his gaze fell to the quivering ground, as if it too were intimidated by the advancing throng of over four hundred men. He raised his head to see Esau emerge from the horde. Jacob limped toward his brother, his prior confidence waning. Bowing seven times, Jacob was unprepared for what happened next. Esau ran to him, not in anger, but embraced him in joy, their tears mingling in God-orchestrated reconciliation. Esau received Jacob's gifts and they went their separate ways, restored.

## Receiver: A Blessed Identity

Jacob would no longer try to manipulate. As he abandoned his need to control, he put himself in a position to receive all God intended. God would continue to lead Jacob, blessing and commending him two more times, and reinforcing his new name, Israel. God would also fulfill Jacob's request, made when he had promised himself to God, to one day return to his father's household in peace.[d] Jacob would see Esau one more time as they journeyed home to bury their father, Isaac.

---

[d] He called the name of that place Bethel, but the name of the city was Luz at first. Then Jacob made a vow, saying, "If God will be with me and will keep me in this way that I go, and will give me bread to eat and clothing to wear, so that I come again to my father's house in peace, then the Lord shall be my God" (Genesis 28:19–21).

God fulfilled another promise as well, one Jacob had made at Bethel, vowing the LORD would be his God. Though Jacob was the one to promise, God was the one to fulfill. Throughout Israel's history, the LORD would be known as the God of Abraham, Isaac, and Jacob. God gave Jacob a new identity, his true identity and purpose for which he was created. And Jacob, renamed Israel by the LORD, would father the twelve tribes of this great nation.

## Receiver: A True Identity

Just as commendation is the key to our development, the source of commendation is the key to its significance. Consider the stolen blessing pronounced by Jacob's father, Isaac. It was a blessing to smell good, a blessing of plenty of grain and wine, a blessing to be served by nations, and more. What's not to like? Why did this blessing fail to take root, to bring peace and security?

The fact is, Jacob obtained it fraudulently. He posed as his brother to procure the coveted blessing. He assumed an alias, attaining an affirmation inconsistent with his identity. Isn't this the root of much of our distress? We wear masks, pretending to be other than ourselves; therefore, whatever commendation we receive is not based in reality. Like our social media posts, we put forth our best images, receiving positive responses to a partial picture. And like a lit candle with too little wick, the glow flickers dimly, then quickly extinguishes.

The masks may not even be products of our own making. Others gladly label us. The labels may be accurate, but either way, we tend to accept them because it is so easy. These labels limit us, however, and like tamper-proof stickers, they are difficult to remove, leaving a distorted mess when we try. Jacob wore the temporary mask of his brother, Esau, but the resulting labels of fraud, imposter, deceiver, and trickster stuck to him like glue—until he encountered God and found joy in His affirmation and pleasure.

## Receiver: A Secure Identity

We discover our true source of identity, purpose, security, and joy in relationship with our Heavenly Father. Listen to Fred Hartley, pastor of One Mission Church in Lilburn, Georgia, describe how our Heavenly Father shatters our labels, glue and all: "Only Father can help you truly be yourself because He fully accepts you and loves you unconditionally. He alone can help you remove your masks—the masks that hide your insecurities and enable you to pose, pretend, and fake it," Hartley says. "He also helps you remove your labels—like Jew, Catholic, Protestant, Muslim, intellectual, scholar, jock, lesbian, gay, straight, OCD, bipolar, addict, alcoholic, druggie, prostitute, or less flattering labels like nerd, geek, dysfunctional, loser, bedwetter, ugly, ignoramus, irreverent, worthless, loser, trash," Hartley continues. "Low self-esteem is the curse of our species; Father is the cure. For this reason, He sees past your labels. He sees you for who you are, and He wants to call you to greatness. He wants to call you child, and He wants to call you mine. He wants you to call Him Father."[10]

Jacob had encountered God previously. But the night before he would meet his brother, Esau, he grabbed hold of Him, refusing to let go, demanding a blessing, a commendation. All of Jacob's labels were torn away, replaced by a new identity. He would now be known as Israel, the chosen nation of God, an identity bestowed by the Father.

There is more. Father has many names, but He took on a new one that night. He would henceforth be known as the God of Abraham, Isaac, and Jacob. Don't miss the significance of this. Jacob did not just receive a new identity from God; he received it in relationship with God. And God, although the same yesterday, today, and tomorrow, the unchangeable Sovereign of all creation, upgraded His identity that night. He defined Himself in relationship with Jacob! This is the triune God, pleasuring in perfect relationship as Father, Son, and Holy Spirit, and He invited Jacob to join in! He invites us as well.

How do we define ourselves? Is our identity based on what we do or on Whose we are? Jacob had no great accomplishments of which to boast. He did not deliver Israel like Moses, or justly rule a kingdom like David. Yet he received his identity in relationship with God and was given the honor to father the twelve tribes of Israel.

What did Jacob discover about God in His journey? He had been taught about God as a child. Yet he chose deception, rather than trust in God, to determine his destiny. He began to believe in God as God revealed Himself at Bethel, protected and delivered Jacob from harm. Yet Jacob only became a receiver when he wrestled with God, demanded God's blessing, and relinquished control. He faced Esau in the lead and trusted God for the outcome. Jacob discovered God's blessing was worthy of his full confidence as he yielded in trust.

As did David Bacon, Jacob received a new identity, no longer defined by deception and manipulation. It was a true identity, that which he was created for. It was a secure identity in relationship with an unchangeable God. And it was a blessed identity as Jacob no longer tried to create his own blessing but sought and trusted in the blessing of God.

How do we try to control our destiny? Do we manipulate, deceive, wear masks in an attempt to create our own blessing?

What if we realized God was waiting to bless us all along, and there is nothing we have to do to earn it?

Alan Wright says it like this. "Some people try hard to succeed so they will feel blessed. Other people try hard to succeed because they already feel blessed. It's the difference between striving and thriving. It's the difference between death and life."[11]

## Receiver: Finding Joy in the Father's Approval

"You're a doctor, aren't you?" A new acquaintance at church thought she had me pegged. I wasn't posing, but the assumed upgrade felt good. I basked in my improved identity for about fifteen seconds before correcting her. My medical expertise ends at applying Band-Aids.

What if we didn't have to hide, to wear masks, to experience joy in God's approval and affirmation? What if God knows everything about us and still offers His commendation? Psalm 139 makes the case: "O Lord, you have searched me and known me! You know when I sit down and when I rise up; you discern my thoughts from afar. You search out my path and my lying down and are acquainted with all my ways" (Psalm 139:1–3). The Psalmist goes on to acknowledge that there is nowhere we can go to hide from God. He is everywhere. Then at the end of the Psalm, he writes this: "Search me, O God, and know my heart! Try me and know my thoughts! And see if there be any grievous way in me, and lead me in the way everlasting!" (Psalm 139:23–24).

It's as if the Psalmist is saying, "OK, God, I give up. You know everything about me anyway, so I can't hide. Show me where I am messing up and how to please you!"

That's the question, isn't it? How do we please God? How do we experience the joy of His pleasure? More on this shortly. But consider this: where do you find the most joy in your relationships?

Think about a time when you felt connected to your parent, spouse, child, significant other, coworker, or friend. What were you doing? The most significant person on Earth for me is my bride of over forty-seven years, Kathy. By the way, she knows everything about me, the good and the bad, and somehow still loves me! I enjoy just being with her and sharing pursuits we both enjoy. For us, this includes camping, hiking, praying, worshiping, and playing with our dog. Sure, we have expectations that we discuss, but our love does not depend on how well we meet them. What brings me the greatest joy is when I see her eyes light up and a big smile spread across her face when I surprise her by bringing her joy. It might be picking out a movie she likes, taking her out to dinner, or an unexpected affirmation. One of her favorites is when I quote Proverbs 31:29, "Many women have done excellently, but you surpass them all!"

It may be similar for you. Relationships are most fulfilling when we seek the other's good, seek to bless. This takes the focus off of us. The delight we experience in pleasing the other brings great joy, not because it props us up but because it deepens the intimacy of the relationship. We are filled with joy and pleasure as we please the ones we love.

God's deepest pleasure is in His son, Jesus. And He wanted to make sure Jesus knew this! He made quite a scene at the beginning of Jesus's public ministry. "And when Jesus was baptized, immediately he went up from the water, and behold, the heavens were opened to him, and he saw the Spirit of God descending like a dove and coming to rest on him; and behold, a voice from heaven said, 'This is my beloved Son, with whom I am well pleased'" (Matthew 3:16–17). And He made a more intimate display toward the end when Jesus transfigured on a mountain while two of His disciples looked on. "He was still speaking when, behold, a bright cloud overshadowed them, and a voice from the cloud said, 'This is my beloved Son, with whom I am well pleased; listen to him'" (Matthew 17:5).

The Greek word *eudokeo* translates as "well pleased," and it is used in both of these passages. It is also used elsewhere. Luke, the author of the eponymous Gospel and the book of Acts, describes the scene at Jesus's birth when an angel appeared to shepherds in the middle of their night watch: "Then suddenly there appeared with the angel a multitude of the heavenly host (angelic army) praising God and saying, 'Glory to God in the highest [heaven], and on earth peace among men with whom He is well-pleased.'" (Luke 2:13–14, Amplified Bible).

Don't miss this. Luke uses the same word to describe God's pleasure in His Son, Jesus, to describe His pleasure in mankind at Jesus's birth. Therefore, the joy we seek in God's approval is greatest when we take great pleasure in His greatest pleasure. Pastor, theologian, and author John Piper sums this up. "If God's pleasure in the Son becomes our pleasure, then the object of our pleasure, Jesus, will be inexhaustible in personal worth."[12]

So, what brings the Father great joy and pleasure and results in His commendation? I'll give you a hint. It starts with Jesus! Let's look at how Jesus opened the eyes of Philip, one of His first chosen disciples, to this truth and what Philip discovered about Jesus that day.

*Whoever has seen me has seen the Father. —Jesus*

—John 14:9

I bless you, dear, beloved seeker,
With an accurate picture of God,
To see Him as He really is,
To reject the lies seeking to corrupt His image,
To discover what touches His heart,
And to realize He is the answer to all you have
been seeking.

# Chapter 3

# It's Not What You Think

*Carefully determine what pleases the Lord.*

—Ephesians 5:10 NLT

*P*hilip's head spun. He had just shared in the Passover meal with Jesus and the other disciples and tried to make sense of all that transpired. Jesus had washed all the disciples' feet and shocked everyone by predicting one of the close-knit group of twelve would betray Him. Each had asked in successive apprehension, "Is it me?"

Judas had made a hurried exit. Now Jesus told them He was going away, that He would come back later, and they should know the way to where He was going! The apprehension turned to confusion. Thomas shrugged, arms outstretched and palms open. "Lord, we don't even know where you are going. How can we know the way?"

Jesus said, "I am the way, and the truth, and the life. No one comes to the Father except through me. If you had known me, you would have known my Father also. From now on you do know him and have seen him."

Philip pleaded, "Lord, show us the Father, and it is enough for us."

Jesus said, "Have I been with you so long, and you still do not know me, Philip? Whoever has seen me has seen the Father. How can you say, 'Show us the Father'? Do you not believe that I am in the Father and the Father is in me?" (John 14:5–10a).

I love this guy, Philip. He responded to Jesus's call immediately, three years earlier. And recognizing Him as the Messiah, he grabbed his friend Nathaniel and brought him to Jesus. But this was different, and confusing. This was bigger than he imagined. He had asked Jesus to reveal the Father, and Jesus said, in effect, "You're looking at Him!"

## Jesus Shows Us What the Father Is Like

It starts with Jesus. This is the launching pad in our desire to please God and to receive His commendation. Listen to American philosopher Dallas Willard when he says, "Until our minds are informed by the right view of God, we cannot put our minds on God in the right way. The problem is so severe that when Jesus came, he essentially said to people, 'Forget everything you think you know about God, and I'm going to tell you what he is really like.'"[13]

What did Philip discover about Jesus that day? An accurate picture of God births both our desire and the right motivation to please Him. Unfortunately, like a fogged-up window, that picture is often distorted. Jesus told Philip, "If you want to know who the Father is, look at me!" Jesus wipes away the foggy film and shows us what the Father is like. Philip discovered the Father's identity in the face of Jesus.

Brennan Manning served as a marine during the Korean War. Then, ordained as a Franciscan priest, he served abroad among the poor. He began his writing in the 1970s after returning to the United States and battling alcoholism, and he is best known for his book *The Ragamuffin Gospel*. He observes, "Thirty-seven years of pastoral experience with Catholics, mainline Protestants, evangelicals, fundamentalists, Seventh Day Adventists, Blacks, whites, Asians, and Hispanics tells me unmistakably that many a believer's perception of God is radically wrong."[14]

What do we get wrong about God that creates such a problem? Pastor Jack Frost's prayer gives us insight: "Father God, I come before You today and humbly ask You to forgive me for judging You wrongly and allowing misrepresentations of who You are to affect my perceptions of You. I have allowed religion, that is based on performance and fear, to color my thoughts toward You. I have sought to please You and gain Your acceptance through my good works. I thought You were angry with me and disappointed in me because I wasn't good enough to deserve Your love. My focus has been on religion and my performance instead of on my relationship with You. Please help me gain a new understanding of Your unconditional love for me."[15]

We can even have the right motivation for pleasing God, but if we are not clear on what actually pleases Him, our picture of Him remains distorted. Our focus on religious rules, regulations, and results ruins an accurate image of God. Fortunately, we can clear up any misconceptions we have of God by looking at Jesus. He is the very image of the Father, His exact representation, fully man and yet fully God![e] So, what brings Jesus pleasure and what He commends is what brings the Father pleasure, gains His approval, and elicits His commendation. We'll look at this

---

[e] "He is the image of the invisible God, the firstborn of all creation" (Colossians 1:15).

shortly. But there is one more thing to know about pleasing God and bringing Him great delight. Though elementary, it is the very cornerstone.

We are so wired with a performance orientation that we've forgotten how to keep it simple. Three days after Jesus fed a crowd of five thousand with five barley loaves and two fish, they followed Him to Capernaum, looking for seconds. Jesus pointed them away from working for food and toward a more eternal perspective. "This is the work of God, that you believe in him whom he has sent" (John 6:29).

Can we grasp the purity of that? There is nothing more pleasing to God, bringing Him greater delight, than believing in and loving Jesus! The crowd still wasn't there. They asked for a dramatic sign that would enable them to believe, apparently forgetting for a moment the previous night's feast. Yet the belief that the Father commends is a simple belief in Jesus, receiving Him whom the Father sent, by faith, without proof or signs. Jesus reinforced this before His arrest and crucifixion as He shared His last words with His disciples. "The Father himself loves you, because you have loved me and have believed that I came from God" (John 16:27).

This is Jesus's word to us as well. We bring the Father the greatest delight, the greatest pleasure, and receive the greatest commendation as we believe in Jesus, love Him, and seek to please Him. So, where does Jesus begin? He begins with the heart.

## Jesus Shows Us What the Father Likes

*For the Lord sees not as man sees: man looks on the outward appearance, but the Lord looks on the heart.*

—1 Samuel 16:7

God is concerned with our internal condition, not our outward appearance. It has always been so. Consider His words to the prophet Samuel as he appraised Jesse's sons to select the next king of Israel. Samuel had been quite impressed with Jesse's first choice, Eliab. God, not so much, as He spoke to Samuel, saying, "Do not look on his appearance or on the height of his stature, because I have rejected him. For the Lord sees not as man sees: man looks on the outward appearance, but the Lord looks on the heart" (1 Samuel 16:7).

Jesse had paraded seven of his sons with the same result before calling his youngest, David, in from the field at Samuel's request. David was the one God chose as the disobedient King Saul's successor.

Like Father, like Son, Jesus has the same perspective. His well-known Mountain Message raises the bar.[f] He equates anger with murder and lust with adultery. Jesus's greatest rebuke describes the Pharisees, the religious leaders of His time, as whitewashed tombs, appearing clean but filled with dead men's bones. Pretty on the outside, ugly on the inside![g]

## What the Father Likes Is Not What You Think

Have you ever thought about what impresses God? I know this question sounds ridiculous. Its absurdity may even amuse you. But admit it. In the back of your mind, you probably have experienced some self-satisfaction in a deed or accomplishment thinking, *I'll bet that made God happy!* I know I have. We may have looked upon a Christian pastor, leader, or teacher

---

[f] The core of Jesus's teaching is contained in the well-known Sermon on the Mount chronicled in Matthew, chapters 5, 6, and 7.
[g] See Matthew 23:27.

with admiration, wishing we could please God like that. Hear what Daniel Henderson, pastor, author, and prayer and renewal leader, has to say:

> It is easy to be caught up in our own religious activities and the familiar bubble of a "Christian culture" and go through the motions with convoluted motives. Like it or not, we are a performance-oriented society, and the church is just as bad, if not worse in some ways, as the world. The "performers" who really know how to produce and put on a good show of talent and entertainment are the headliners at most Christian gatherings. They may be pastors, authors, musicians, comedians, businessmen, or just ordinary people with a sizzling story. Either way you cut it, sizzle sells over substance.[16]

I love the movie *Chariots of Fire*, featuring Ian Charleson as Eric Liddell, Scottish rugby player, sprinter, 1924 Olympic 400-meter champion, and missionary to China. A favorite scene depicts Eric's sister Jenny criticizing him for his obsession with running when, like his father, he could be serving God in China. He replies in amusement, "I believe God made me for China, but He also made me fast. And when I run, I feel His pleasure."[17] Imagine that. In Eric's eyes, God was just as pleased with his athletic endeavors as with his missionary service.

Duncan Hamilton, author of *For the Glory*, describes how the real Eric's wife, Florence, responded to the movie. "Yes, she found the interest around the film 'kinda fun.' Yes, she thought Ian Charleson's portrayal caught the 'spirit' of Liddell's personality. No, the script hadn't quite captured him completely. The cinema version was 'a bit too solemn' and 'a little too preachy.'"[18]

Eric never took himself too seriously, and Florence enjoyed his humor and playful side. She also admired his integrity. Hamilton describes Florence's observations: "A lot of people pretend to be what they are not. They superficially put on an act designed to impress or flatter. They behave in a way that their social antennae tell them will suit either the company or the circumstances of the moment."

Hamilton points out that Florence knew Liddell wasn't like this, that he was just himself and nothing more. "He didn't change his accent or his manner, and he didn't compromise his beliefs so that a dinner-table audience or a roomful of strangers gained a false impression of him," Hamilton says. "The boldest lines of the sketch Florence always drew of him conveyed his gentleness and tolerance."[19]

Eric Liddell refused lucrative endorsements resulting from his athletic success. His goal was to glorify Christ in all he did. He took great joy in bringing Christ pleasure, and Christ took great pleasure in what brought Eric joy. He would later serve in China as a missionary and would die there during the Japanese occupation in the Second Sino-Japanese War. Notice Eric did not say, "When I win, I feel His pleasure." Instead, he simply stated, "When I run, I feel His pleasure." It is not in great accomplishments but rather in a life tuned to Him that Jesus takes pleasure.

Is it difficult to believe God takes pleasure in the joy you find in pursuing a passion? We recently had a town hall meeting at our church where the congregation interviewed potential leadership candidates on their qualifications and vision. Many questions were offered and answered well. Toward the end of the meeting our pastor's wife asked, "What do you do for fun?" I thought it was a great question, which temporarily stumped the candidates. One mentioned painting, another sailing. The third, who raises cattle, offered, "I enjoy cows, from the castrating to the eating!" Hilarity ensued.

A significant aspect of Eric Liddell's personality that brought God pleasure was his sense of humor and playfulness as previously described by his wife. God is the author of humor and takes joy in our participation in sanctified humor. Charles Spurgeon, dubbed the Prince of Preachers, was known for it. The Spurgeon Center posts that "he never went out of his way to make a joke, or to avoid one" and that "Spurgeon's playful personality surfaced in his sermons." Once, when admonished for making a joke in the pulpit, Spurgeon said, "If you had known how many others I kept back, you would not have found fault with that one."[20]

I identify with Eric Liddell. I have always loved speed. As a toddler, I would race down our hallway on all fours, sometimes with nothing touching the carpet. I ran track in high school and was co-captain of the team in my senior year. My passion involves every form of transportation, including bicycles, motorcycles, sports cars, trains, airplanes, and sailboats—and the faster the better. All within legal limits, of course, although I have had the privilege of meeting the occasional state trooper. Some of the most passionate servants of God I know are also passionate about golf, an avocation lost on me. Golf carts just aren't that fast!

God loves passion, humor, and authenticity. He is revulsed by lukewarm apathy, self-seriousness, and hypocrisy. He takes joy in those who pursue Him, His Kingdom, and life passionately; do not separate the sacred from the secular; and seek to honor Him in all they do.

## What Jesus Commends: Knowing Him

*So now faith, hope, and love abide, these three; but the greatest of these is love.*

—1 Corinthians 13:13

There is much written on what pleases God, what He desires to see in the lives of those who follow Christ. But if we want to know what touches Jesus's heart, what brings Him pleasure, then look at what causes Him to stop in His tracks, to stand up, to take notice, to comment, and to commend. In most cases, those He commends do not possess great accomplishments. In fact, Jesus rejected those who sought access to the Kingdom of Heaven based on their deeds. Listen to the words from His Mountain Message. "Not everyone who says to me, 'Lord, Lord,' will enter the Kingdom of Heaven, but the one who does the will of my Father who is in heaven. On that day many will say to me, 'Lord, Lord, did we not prophesy in your name, and cast out demons in your name, and do many mighty works in your name?' And then will I declare to them, 'I never knew you; depart from me, you workers of lawlessness'" (Matthew 7:21–23).

On the contrary, none of those Jesus commends are actively seeking His commendation. Their actions flow from their hearts. And the actions of our hearts are what touches God's heart. Jesus describes this scene at the final judgment in Matthew 25:34–40:

> Then the King will say to those on his right, "Come, you who are blessed by my Father, inherit the kingdom prepared for you from the foundation of the world. For I was hungry and you gave me food, I was thirsty and you gave me drink, I was a stranger and you welcomed me, I was naked and you clothed me, I was sick and you visited me, I was in prison and you came to me." Then the righteous will answer him, saying, "Lord, when did we see you hungry and feed you, or thirsty and give you drink? And when did we see you a stranger and welcome you, or naked and clothe you? And when did we

see you sick or in prison and visit you?" And the King will answer them, "Truly, I say to you, as you did it to one of the least of these my brothers, you did it to me."

\*     \*     \*

"You know me. Great will be your reward." These were words spoken over me during an unusual job interview in 2008. We were in conversations with a new ministry regarding corporate aviation services we had been asked to provide. Rather than meeting with an HR department, we met with a pastor who prayed over us to discern God's calling. This stunned me. Could it be that, although I had no great accomplishments and had pursued a secular career, God was pleased with me, and my reward was based on knowing Him?

There was more. The pastor went on to declare that God was calling me to be a pastor, not to the healthy sheep but to the broken and hurting sheep, and I was to obey Him. The new ministry that had interviewed us never developed, and in the following year, when the 2009 recession hit, my aviation job ended, and I was unemployed for the next year. It was during this time, while our church provided a hot meal at our local Salvation Army, that I was asked to lead the devotional. God told me to keep coming back once a week. I fell in love with those we served, with hopes, dreams, and needs no different from my own. The Salvation Army chaplains asked me to continue offering devotionals, which I did throughout that year. They also asked me to participate in their retirement ceremony in April of 2010.

Over the next five years, I would serve two different mission organizations, one as staff pastor and the other as director of the prayer ministry. During this time, I had the opportunity to serve with ministry teams in Haiti, Jamaica, India, and Mexico and developed deep friendships along the way. A small hundred-year-old country church also invited me to serve as their pastor over the same period. I came to love these dear people as well. Oh, and the first pastor of this church was a man named Bishop Milton Wright. He had two sons named Orville and Wilbur who moved to Dayton and opened a bicycle shop! Did I mention, God has a great sense of humor?

Even after returning to aviation in 2015, I still feel called to the hurting and broken. God provided an opportunity to join a ministry team serving pastors in South Africa and Malawi in 2017 and later to serve on ministry teams in our local jail. But let me be clear. None of this merited God's approval. His commendation was based on knowing Him and pursuing Him as He revealed Himself in every relationship and endeavor. The opportunities to join Him in loving and serving those He loves are merely the outflow of knowing Him and His heart.

What did I discover about Jesus during this time? As our knowledge of Jesus deepens, we become more like Him. We are attracted to those to whom He is attracted. We find joy in that which brings Him joy. And He takes pleasure in what brings us joy. This is a shared joy that is real, satisfying, and lasting. It is joy doubling down, His joy as He commends, and our joy as we receive His commendation. Knowing Jesus takes many forms. Let's look further into what He commends.

## Faith, Hope, and Love

There is a common distinction characterizing the actions of those Jesus commends. Faith is the foundation, but these actions also include one of the overlapping categories of hope or love. Picture faith as the belief in the unseen God that causes us to act. Picture hope as the quality that enables us to persevere, to not give up. And picture love as the only commendable motivation for our action. Consider some of those Jesus encountered. A Roman centurion showed great faith in trusting Jesus to heal his servant remotely; a woman with a hemorrhage lasting twelve years showed great hope, pushing through a crowd to touch Jesus's robe; and a poor, elderly widow showed great love with two small coins she offered to God. Each recognized a unique aspect of Jesus's identity and nature. Each responded differently to what they saw. We will look at what Jesus commends through their eyes.

Now that our picture of the Father and of His Son, Jesus, is clarifying, we see a God worthy of our faith and trust. As we continue our journey, let's take a deeper look at faith and why it is the essential foundation for pleasing God. Strap in and hang on.

> *By faith Enoch was taken up so that he should not see death, and he was not found, because God had taken him. Now before he was taken he was commended as having pleased God.*

> —Hebrews 11:5

I bless you, dear, beloved seeker,

That having been taken,

With an accurate picture of Him,

You discover He can be trusted completely.

I bless you to bring Him pleasure,

As you exercise your growing faith,

And to find your joy in His approval, affirmation, and pleasure,

As He responds to your trust.

# Section 2

···•✦•···

# Faith

# Chapter 4

## Faith: The Catalyst for Action

*And without faith it is impossible to please him, for*
*whoever would draw near to God must believe that*
*he exists and that he rewards those who seek him.*

—Hebrews 11:6 ESV

Faith is a belief in the unseen yet personal and all-powerful God. It is a firm conviction that trusts in His love and His intentions toward us for our best, which leads us to action. Faith, acting on what a person knows of God, is the essence of what pleases God and receives His commendation. The author of Hebrews is more direct in our title verse. Faith is essential for pleasing God.

So how do we begin to believe in an unseen God? Consider the following progression. Faith forms as God reveals Himself and gives us grace to believe. He gives us tests, invitations to trust Him. He then rewards that trust by showing who He is and what He can do. To put it simply, God initiates and invites, we respond, and He rewards. Let's see what this looks like. We'll see how faith forms, tests, invites, and rewards.

## Faith Forms and Tests

It was the spring of 1975 when I received the letter from Rosemead School of Psychology. I would be graduating from Ohio State University in June and had applied to Rosemead's graduate program in Christian counseling, expectantly awaiting their response, sure of God's lead. The day the letter came was a bad day. The rejection was bad enough, but my anger kindled at the last sentence. "We hope you will take this as God's will for your life."

"How can it be God's will that only one hundred people a year gain acceptance to a graduate program in Christian counseling?" I yelled, more at the trite platitude than the potential dearth of faith-based therapists. I had known God for three and a half years. My faith formed and grew as I experienced His answers to prayer. But this was new. I sulked. The Holy Spirit graciously interrupted my pity party.

"Aren't you to thank God in all things?"

The Holy Spirit has a gentle way of giving me a kick in the rear when needed! Like a dog dragged to a bath by its collar, I dropped to my knees, joined by my wife, Kathy. "I don't know why I'm doing this, Father, but thank you for this letter."

The phone rang an hour later. "This is Dr. Bill Donaldson with the Religious Consultation and Research Society in Atlanta." (The institution is now called Richmont Graduate University.) "We are a new graduate program in Christian counseling and would like to invite you to apply." Dr. Donaldson went on to describe their partnership with Georgia State University. And the kicker? Rosemead had given them my name!

I applied and was accepted. Kathy was subsequently invited by an Atlanta company for a job interview. She returned empty-handed. It was now a week before class was to start. We had enough cash for first quarter's tuition, a U-Haul, apartment deposit, and first month's rent. But still no employment offers. This is where it got real. How much do we trust God? Do we take the phone call and acceptance as God's invitation? Within two weeks of our arrival, we both had jobs that more than covered our needs. I would graduate with two degrees from Georgia State University three years later, and Kathy would remain with the same employer for the next twenty-seven years.

Faith starts with what God reveals of Himself. As we understand His love, we gain the confidence in Him to act in trust. This act is often a simple step of obedience. Faith is a powerful conviction without which we cannot please God. But faith is a noun. Trust is often a verb.

Brennan Manning describes this relationship between faith and trust. He says that "we would discover with alarm that the essence of biblical faith lies in trusting God." Manning goes on to say that "as Marcus Borg has noted, 'The first is a matter of the head, the second a matter of the heart. The first can leave us unchanged, the second intrinsically brings change.'"[21]

I like the phrase *act of trust*. The phrase *act of faith* can imply that faith belief is sufficient action in and of itself. *Act of trust* implies an action taken, based on faith, which is doomed to failure unless God acts. But how do we gain such conviction to take such a great step? God reveals enough about Himself to enable us to take a small step at first. An act of trust often starts with simple obedience. As God responds, this leads to a deeper understanding of His love, trustworthiness, and power, allowing us to take even greater steps of faith.

Our move to Atlanta was one of our first major experiences with faith. God responded quickly to our initial ninety-pound weakling act of obedience in the prayer of thanks. Subsequent invitations to trust have, like an athlete who gradually increases lifting weight, involved ever greater intervals of wait. God does not always answer in the way or time frame I expect, but He does answer in a way resulting in a deeper peace and confidence in Him.

## Faith Responds to an Invitation

Peter stretched and massaged his sore arms as the storm-spit spray soaked him. The Sea of Galilee is shallow, easily disturbed by local weather, and it had been a long, wet, tumultuous, night, pulling head to wind against increasing seas in the small craft. Jesus had just fed five thousand people with five loaves and two small fish and ordered His disciples to cross on ahead, alone. Dawn approached with little progress, and as the wind and waves increased, so did the disciples' fear. The fear climaxed in the disciples' screams as a ghostly figure appeared out of the spray, walking on water. The figure took on human form and definition as it approached.

"Take heart; it is I. Do not be afraid," said Jesus in response to the disciples' cries.

"Lord, if it is you, command me to come to you on the water," said Peter.

"Come!" said Jesus. Peter put one hand on the gunwale and vaulted over the side, amazed his feet found a firm landing as he walked toward Jesus.[h]

Faith is the grace to receive from God, initiated by God, and His invitation to draw near to Him resulting in absolute trust in Him. Faith in Jesus, evidenced in trust, drew Kathy and me to

---

[h] The account of Jesus walking on the water and included dialogue is taken from Matthew 14:22–33.

Atlanta. Faith in Jesus, evidenced in trust, drew Peter out of the boat. Peter's encounter with the foaming waves required a much greater faith than my encounter with mere puddles. But notice that both my experience and Peter's required an invitation, one that Peter wisely requested. And Peter RSVP'd immediately when Jesus said "Come." It would have been foolish presumption to act without Jesus's summons. It would have been foolish on my part to move to Atlanta without God's invitation. But when Jesus says "Come," it is foolish to refuse. The invitation and the faith to receive and respond do not originate in us. It is a gift of the grace of God. He starts where we are and builds faith within us as we act.

What did Kathy and I learn about Jesus in our move to Atlanta? What did Peter learn about Jesus in his encounter on the lake? When Jesus invites, He can be trusted fully with our steps of faith, even when we falter. Faith in Jesus is never misplaced.

## Faith Is Rewarded and a Reward

Don't miss the implication of the second part of this chapter's title verse, "For whoever would draw near to God must believe that he exists and that he rewards those who seek him." The rewards of faith are for those who seek God. A profound dynamic takes place when we exercise faith in God. As we seek Him, He commends and rewards our act of trust. As we step toward Him in faith, we bring Him great pleasure. And as He responds, we experience great joy. This joy is not just in the reward of His answer to our trust, but our joy in the reward of the intimacy we experience as He opens our eyes to see more of Him.

We don't do this perfectly. Consider Peter as he falters in his steps toward Jesus, how he exhibited great trust, knowing that even if he were to fail, Jesus would rescue him. Brennan Manning explains, "When we wander off the path, that trust pulls us back; and we do not flinch, hesitate, or worry about being unwelcome in the Father's arms. No matter where we are on the journey, we have a quiet confidence that our trust in God's love gives God immense pleasure."[22]

\* \* \*

A young child, seeing her daddy at the bottom of the stairway, descends to meet him. She stops suddenly, two stairs up, and smiles. Her daddy stretches his arms as she giggles in anticipation. She launches herself into orbit, splashing down in the ocean of her daddy's enveloping love as she hugs his neck. He belly-laughs as she squeals. She runs back up the stairs, this time to the fourth step. "Do it again, Daddy!"

Can we sense the reward of joy they both experience? The bonding? The trust to now double down? Brennan Manning describes this pleasure: "The splendor of a human heart which trusts that it is loved gives God more pleasure than Westminster Cathedral, the Sistine Chapel, Beethoven's Ninth Symphony, Van Gogh's Sunflowers, the sight of ten thousand butterflies in flight, or the scent of a million orchids in bloom. Trust is our gift back to God, and he finds it so enchanting that Jesus died for love of it."[23]

## Faith Is the Common Thread

Remember our story of Jacob, how he had no great accomplishments but found himself defined by his relationship with God, along with Abraham and Isaac? What was so special about Jacob that resulted in God's commendation? Alan Wright offers us insight from Hebrews 11, known as the "Faith Hall of Fame."

This faith Hall of Fame list also includes Moses, Daniel, David, Samson, and the great prophets. There are no surprises there, except one: "By faith Jacob, when dying, blessed each of the sons of Joseph, bowing in worship over the head of his staff" (v. 21). Old Jacob made the list? The conniving, confused deceiver found a place next to Samson and Moses and David? An old man leaning on his staff and speaking blessing made the famous Hebrews 11 chapter? Is blessing someone an act of faith on par with the Red Sea parting and Jericho walls tumbling? Absolutely.[24]

This concept of faith is the common thread running through the tapestry of these stories that Jesus commends as well. In fact, it is faith that most often elicits a response from Jesus, a verbal commendation, blessing, or an act of healing. And it is a lack of faith that most often receives a rebuke. We will notice each person Jesus commends has a different awareness of Him. One knows Him intimately; others, sharing a common heritage, know well of His reputation. And others, completely isolated by geography and race, have only heard stories of Him. Yet it is these who often display the greatest faith. Each one acts on what they know of Jesus as He reveals Himself uniquely according to their need. And each of these express their faith differently, receiving the reward of His particular commendation. We'll look next at a Roman commander, one who knew of Jesus only by reputation as a rabbi new in town but was driven to an encounter with Him in desperation, and experienced joy in God's pleasure as Jesus acknowledged his faith and responded to his request. Let's see what he discovered about Jesus.

*And to the centurion Jesus said, "Go; let it be done for you as you have believed." And the servant was healed at that very moment.*

—Matthew 8:13

I bless you, beloved, powerful one,
To see Jesus's greater power and authority,
To experience His peace in the storm of His holiness,
Even as you are aware of your unholiness,
And to receive His answer,
And commendation,
As you believe Him for the impossible,
And find your joy in His approval, affirmation,
and pleasure.

# Chapter 5

## A Great Faith

*Blessed are the poor in spirit, for theirs is the kingdom
of heaven. —Jesus*

—Matthew 5:3

*F*lavius gazed over the lake, reflecting on life even as the still
water reflected the azure sky and clouds above. The blue-
and-white patchwork mixed with the melodic cries of gulls and
the scent of the fresh sea breeze created a delicious banquet for
the senses. He liked Capernaum. Sure, his chances of promotion
were slim, and he would likely retire at his present rank of centurion. But it was a peaceful town, far from the hotbed of Jerusalem,
and after all, he had a small villa on the Sea of Galilee and a warm
relationship with the local Jewish population. And he had never
been forced to call upon the men he commanded to take up arms
against the locals.

He liked the Jews as well. They had something, or rather,
someone. The God they worshipped was One, far different than
the myriad gods of Rome. They were devoted to their God with

an affection that gave meaning to their lives, a devotion that stirred something deep within Flavius's soul, awakening a yearning, a long-dormant emotion, as one roused from a deep, prolonged slumber.

And this yearning had led him to build a synagogue for the Jews in which they could worship their God. Perhaps he had built it for himself as well. He would often eavesdrop on their gatherings and felt something whenever near. Not the man-made glory and frenzied activity of the temples of Rome but rather a solemn stillness, a tangible presence that moved him.

Yes, it was a good life, and becoming increasingly interesting. A young rabbi had recently taken up residence in Capernaum and was attracting a following. Initially, Flavius raised his guard, but the rumors of healings, miracles, the authority of His teaching, and the peaceful nature of his followers soon dispelled his concerns. He would have to meet this Jesus Bar-Joseph and see for himself.

The approach of one of Flavius's soldiers interrupted his reverie. His day was about to take a turn for the worse. Flavius tensed as he saw the grim expression on the man's face. "It's Lucius. Come quickly," pleaded the soldier. "He's burning up!"

Flavius gathered his cloak and ran toward the house, the soldier hurrying behind. Lucius was Flavius's favorite servant. But more than a servant, he had become the most trusted member of his household, managing all of Flavius's domestic affairs. Lucius had appeared unusually tired recently, and his health had deteriorated significantly.

Flavius rushed to Lucius's room, stopping short at his appearance. Dark circles ringed Lucius's eyes. The sound of shallow, labored breathing assaulted Flavius's ears. Lucius's pale, grayish skin appeared like cold ashes remaining from a once bright and glowing fire. A stifling smell with which Flavius was quite familiar filled the room. It was the smell of decay that he had encountered on the field of battle hours after the fighting had ceased.

Flavius teared as Lucius turned toward him, his eyes brightening like two dying embers' last glow. Flavius knew what he had to do. If he were ever to meet this new rabbi, it must be now. He turned to his soldier. "Quick, go to the Jewish elders. Implore them to bring Jesus. Lucius is dying!" Flavius turned toward his servant as the soldier hurried away. He took Lucius's hand as the servant slowly drifted off to sleep. "It will be OK," he whispered. "It will be OK. Jesus is coming."

Flavius slowly stood and left the room. He walked outside and gazed over the lake. Where had the words come from, "It will be ok"? Mere dreaming, like a starving man bending to grasp a handful of straw, hoping to find a few kernels of wheat? Or was it something more? Something that he couldn't quite place? How could he be sure? How could he know? He cried out, "God of the Jews, if you are real, show me now!"

As Flavius pondered, he heard the soldier's voice, faint at first, then growing in volume as he approached. "He is coming. Jesus is coming. The elders are bringing Him now and He is not far away."

*He is not far away.* These words gave Flavius great hope. He felt an anticipation, but more than that, a Holy Presence that enveloped him with a calmness and peace previously unknown.

But an increasing apprehension suddenly overwhelmed him. It was not a sense of apprehension concerning Lucius. No, this was a sense of apprehension concerning himself. A sense of an approaching power, of awe over something much greater than himself, as the approach of a distant storm, with towering dark clouds and flashes of lightning but not yet audible thunder, warns of that to come. And just as an approaching storm comes with an irresistible power, so a divine authority accompanied Jesus's approach, which overwhelmed Flavius, and before which his knees weakened. The realization of the stark limits of his own authority and power battered him as he became increasingly aware of the authority of Jesus. He realized he was about to encounter the Holy, and his own unholiness terrified him.

The wind increased, and as Flavius gazed over the lake, the developing whitecaps mimicked his dread. He turned to his soldier, the pronounced urgency evident in his voice: "Quickly, go to Jesus and tell him, 'Lord, do not trouble yourself, for I am not worthy to have you come under my roof. Therefore I did not presume to come to you. But say the word, and let my servant be healed. For I too am a man set under authority, with soldiers under me: and I say to one, 'Go,' and he goes; and to another, 'Come,' and he comes; and to my servant, 'Do this,' and he does it" (Luke 7:6b-8).

Flavius walked slowly back to the house as the soldier ran to intercept Jesus. He gazed back over the lake, taking in the whitecaps one last time before turning to enter his home. A strong breeze from behind propelled him as he made his way to where Lucius lay. But Lucius was not in bed. He stood, his face and complexion radiant, his eyes like glowing embers fanned back into flame. Flavius smiled as he embraced his servant. He was not surprised. He would not meet Jesus today after all. He never heard Jesus utter the words commending him to His entourage. "I tell you; not even in Israel have I found such faith!" (Luke 7:9b).

Though he would not meet Jesus, Flavius had encountered Him. An encounter that left him with such an understanding of Jesus's authority that he exhibited a faith greater than that found in all of Israel. A faith Jesus both commended and rewarded.

## Jesus Commends a Recognition of His Authority

What did Flavius recognize about Jesus that day, and what was the source of his faith? Great faith requires an accurate view of Jesus. For us, the recognition of Jesus's authority as the Son of God is the foundation for faith. Flavius may not have recognized Jesus as the Jewish Messiah and probably was not aware of Jesus's divinity as the Son of God. So, what did he see? Although he may not have recognized its source, Flavius recognized and put his faith in Jesus's great authority and power, and Jesus commended him for it.

Whenever Jesus taught, those listening perceived a difference. He exuded an authority not found in the teachings of the Jewish religious leaders of the day. These leaders were offended by it. The crowds flocked to it. But what enabled this Roman military leader to get it? Flavius was a man familiar with authority. He respected it, wielded it, and submitted to it. Authority was a quality Flavius identified with, and it was the primary quality he recognized in Jesus.

When we recognize Jesus's authority, it is a sure sign we can submit to God's authority. If we have a problem with authority, it is a sure sign we are not under God's authority. The Jewish religious leaders challenged Jesus's authority, even when He healed a man born lame to demonstrate it—a clear sign they were not under God's authority. But there is more to Flavius's response of faith and what he saw that day that received Jesus's commendation.

# A Recognition of Jesus's Authority Reveals Our Great Poverty

Great faith also requires an accurate view of ourselves. Countless Roman military leaders were impressed with their own importance, which obscured an accurate view of Jesus. Flavius was overcome by a powerful sense of Jesus's holiness. As Jesus neared, Flavius's sense of His holiness grew. The more the sense of Jesus's holiness grew, the greater the experience of Flavius's unholiness, moral poverty, and unworthiness grew. Jesus commends a great faith born out of a humble recognition of our own poverty and unworthiness. Flavius understood this.

Jesus described those with this sense of unworthiness as being "poor in spirit" and, in His Mountain Message, commended them as worthy to receive the Kingdom of God.[i] This type of humility evidenced itself in the love Flavius had for the Jews and in his care for his servant. As was true of the Pharisees, the focus on religious rules and observances can stifle both faith and tenderness that would recognize Jesus's compassion. A heart of compassion will recognize Jesus's compassion.

\*　　\*　　\*

Flavius's humility would not allow him to approach Jesus directly. However, humility-based faith can also express itself in boldness to intrude upon His Presence. What did a brash Canaanite woman see in Jesus that fueled her approach? And how will Jesus respond to her temerity? It may not be how we think! Let's see next.

---

[i] "Blessed are the poor in spirit, for theirs is the kingdom of heaven." —Jesus, Matthew 5:3.

*If you then, who are evil, know how to give good gifts to your children, how much more will your Father who is in heaven give good things to those who ask him! —Jesus*

—Matthew 7:11

I bless you, dear, beloved, desperate one,
With the boldness to approach Jesus with your need.
I bless you with a faith,
To recognize His invitation,
Even in His seeming indifference.
I bless you with the anticipation, not of entitlement,
But of His mercy available to all.
I bless you with the persistence to keep asking,
Until you receive His answer,
And I bless you to receive joy,
In His commendation,
For your great faith.

# Chapter 6

## A Bold Faith

*And I tell you, ask, and it will be given to you; seek, and
you will find; knock, and it will be opened to you. For
everyone who asks receives, and the one who seeks finds,
and to the one who knocks it will be opened. —Jesus*

—Luke 11:9–10

*What is He doing here?* Thalia pondered as she listened to
the rumor. There were reports of Jesus entering a house
with His disciples near Zarephath, in the region of Tyre and
Sidon. *Highly unlikely,* she reflected, contemplating the long
history of animosity between the Canaanites and the Jews.
*And yet, why not?* Thalia had also heard rumors of Jesus feeding five thousand people with only a few loaves and a couple
of fish in Gennesaret just last week. *If Jesus were seeking relief
from the throng after such an event, this would be the perfect
place to flee. Tyre and Sidon would be the last place the Jews
would look for Him.*

"Could it actually be true?" Thalia said aloud, and then quickly glanced around to see if she had been overheard as she weighed the possibilities. If it were true, this was an opportunity. And however unlikely this rumor might be, Thalia was just desperate enough to act on it.

Thalia's face fell as she looked at the corner of the room. There sat her daughter, rocking rapidly back and forth on the floor. Her blank stare transformed into a contorted jeer as Thalia caught her eye. Her rocking stopped momentarily as a deep, resonant laugh, far alien to the nature of a six-year-old girl, terrorized Thalia. She turned away, reverting to her blank expression, resuming her rocking.

Demon possession manifested occasionally in this region, still characterized by the worship of Ba'al, Ashtoreth, and other gods and goddesses. Yes, Thalia was desperate, and if there was a chance that Jesus was in the area, she would find Him. And if what people were saying about Him was true, there might be hope. Thalia took one last look at her daughter, and leaving her in the care of her sister, hurried into the street.

It did not take long. A person of Jesus's stature, no matter how innocuously He arrived, did not escape notice. A sudden wave of anxiety enveloped Thalia like a thick cloak, though it provided no warmth as she shivered. *Who is this man?* Thalia slouched as she approached the house. And there He stood in the courtyard, seeming tall and imposing, surrounded by His disciples. She caught His eyes and blurted, "Have mercy on me, O Lord, Son of David; my daughter is severely oppressed by a demon!"

Jesus stared at her, eyes questioning.

Thalia straightened and cried out again. "Have mercy on me, O Lord, Son of David; my daughter is severely oppressed by a demon."

A disciple grabbed Jesus's tunic, clearly irritated as were the others at this Gentile's interruption of their retreat. "Send her away, for she is crying out after us."

Jesus, however, fixed His gaze on Thalia and said softly, "I was sent only to the lost sheep of the house of Israel."

Thalia's hopes withered. She stiffened, as if slapped, and stared open-mouthed at Jesus. But there was something in His look, and the fact that Jesus had not turned away. Was it a look of incredulity at this affront? No... it was something else, a look of... invitation, anticipation, as if He expected her to respond. Emboldened, Thalia came toward Him, falling on her knees. "Lord, help me," she cried, then waited.

Jesus answered, "It is not right to take the children's bread and throw it to the dogs."

And there it was, that look again. Why did He not just turn and walk away? What was He waiting for? Thalia suddenly remembered a story she had heard. It was true that the Jews despised Gentiles, but something had happened a long time ago, in this very place.

There was a story of a local widow, here in Zarephath, who had used her last provisions to prepare a meal for the Jewish prophet Elijah and saw her provisions multiply—oil and grain that never ran out. And she recalled more. This widow brought her child, her only son who had died, to Elijah, and he restored his life! Thalia smiled at this and looked at Jesus. "Yes, Lord, yet even the dogs eat the crumbs that fall from their master's table."

Jesus grinned broadly. His eyes softened yet blazed like the rising sun exploding over the horizon. "O woman, great is your faith! Be it done for you as you desire."

Thalia jumped with delight and ran back to her house, confident of what she would find. She was not disappointed. Tears of joy streamed as she heard the words "Amma, Amma!" and her little daughter ran and jumped into her arms![j]

## Jesus Commends a Cry for Mercy

Jesus commends great faith fueled by a humble recognition of our need for mercy. What amazes here is Thalia, her status as not only a Canaanite but as a woman, would have had truly little knowledge of Jesus and would have been the least permitted to approach Him. Yet she acted boldly on what little she knew and sought Him out, refusing to let go. Her boldness was not from a sense of entitlement. It was from a recognition of Jesus's mercy. Don't let this pass us by. If we think we do not deserve Jesus's commendation, we are right. But that has nothing to do with it. Thalia did not either. But she saw who Jesus was and would not let go of Him. She would not take no for an answer.

There is a progression to a transforming encounter with Jesus. It begins with a desperation that sees God as our only hope. It is born of humility that realizes we bring nothing to the table, we do not deserve an answer, and we are not entitled to a response.

Jim Cymbala, pastor of the well-known Brooklyn Tabernacle, tells of a transformational moment early in the church's history. The congregation was struggling to pay its bills, and Jim was trying to figure out how to minister to the small inner-city gathering. "On one of those Sunday nights early on, I was so depressed by what I saw—and even more by what I felt in my spirit—that I literally could not preach. Five minutes into my sermon, I began choking on the words. Tears filled my eyes. Gloom engulfed me. All I could say to the people was 'I'm sorry... I... I... can't preach

---

[j] The story of the Canaanite woman and included dialogue is taken from Matthew 15:21–28.

in this atmosphere... Something is terribly wrong... I don't know what to say—I can't go on... If we don't see God help us, I don't know..."[25]

Jim asked his wife to play a song and invited those gathered to come to the front of the church. People sang along to "I Need Thee Every Hour" and began to pray, when a young usher came running forward in tears; he confessed to stealing money from the collection and promised to never do it again. Jim was amazed. He did not need to confront. God brought this all to light. He describes this spiritual breakthrough. "That evening, when I was at my lowest, confounded by obstacles, bewildered by the darkness that surrounded us, unable to even continue preaching, I discovered an astonishing truth: God is attracted to weakness," Jim said. "He can't resist those who humbly and honestly admit how desperately they need him. Our weakness, in fact, makes room for his power."[26]

Fred Hartley describes this principle well. "It is only when you and I recognize our utter hopelessness, lostness, incompetence, and utter ineptitude that we become candidates for God's redeeming grace."[27]

As we approach Jesus with the reality of who we are in humility, we then progress to seeing Jesus for who He is, both His power to answer and His mercy and grace toward us.

## Jesus Commends Those Who Recognize Who He Is

It was the winter of 2020, and I was eating my dinner alone at Palm Beach International Airport, waiting for my flight home. I heard the voice first. "Dave, is that you?" I turned to see a pastor friend under whom I had served in ministry between 2010 and 2012 and had not seen since. My face lit up in joy as we hugged! We had booked the same flight and spent the next two hours catching up as the flight attendant graciously allowed him to join me in the exit row.

We all love recognition! I was not particularly hiding but was wearing a cowboy hat, so I was surprised I was identified. Jesus delighted in recognition as well. Not the recognition of public acclaim but a recognition of his identity. He did not seek to announce his identity but took joy in those to whom the Father revealed Him. What did Thalia recognize about Jesus that day? What did she see that ignited her boldness and persistence? Thalia certainly perceived Jesus as merciful, which drew her in. What is more, she addressed Jesus as "Son of David," a Messianic title. Incredulously, this Canaanite woman, an unschooled foreigner, got it when the religious leaders of Israel, trained in the scriptures, did not. When Jesus sees this recognition, He always sees it as a sign that God is working, that the Father is revealing Himself and the Son. He particularly enjoys when those who should be the last to see it, do. We can hear the delight in His words as He speaks.

"At that time Jesus declared, 'I thank you, Father, Lord of heaven and earth, that you have hidden these things from the wise and understanding and revealed them to little children; yes, Father, for such was your gracious will. All things have been handed over to me by my Father, and no one knows the Son except the Father, and no one knows the Father except the Son and anyone to whom the Son chooses to reveal him'" (Matthew 11:25–27).

As we increasingly discover more of Jesus's character as a man, recognize His divinity and authority, and comprehend His love, mercy, grace, and power, as revealed by the Father, we bring Him great pleasure. This is what Thalia saw, which led her to the final step in a transforming encounter with Jesus, approaching Him boldly.

## Jesus Commends Those Who Approach Him Boldly

Jesus commends and responds to those who see Him for who He is, approach Him humbly yet boldly, and do not let go until they receive an answer. This begs the question, why does Jesus seem to be reluctant to answer, even seem to ignore Thalia? Jesus's disciples had just begged Him to send her away. He addressed her, "I was sent only to the lost sheep of the house of Israel."

We can just picture the disciples looking at her and saying, "Yeah, you heard Him. Scram!" But Thalia persists, causing Jesus to respond.

"It is not right to take the children's bread and throw it to the dogs."

Now the disciples rouse. "Yeah, you tell her Jesus!" they say as they fist bump and high five each other.

But Thalia continues, "Yes, Lord, yet even the dogs eat the crumbs that fall from their master's table," earning both a commendation and response from Jesus.

"O woman, great is your faith! Be it done for you as you desire."

The disciples' mouths fall open. "Wait, what?"

What is going on here; what just happened? Perhaps some context will give us a clue. Recently the disciples had also asked Jesus to send others away. They had faced a hungry crowd of five thousand who followed Jesus's every word yet had no food to give them. Jesus had declined their request and instructed them to feed the crowd. When all they could find were five loaves and two fish, Jesus created a banquet, out of a child's meal!

Might Jesus have been testing His disciples, waiting to see how they would respond as He stepped back? Would they take the initiative to extend mercy to this persistent foreigner? Would they object to His refusals? And would they learn from His delight in Thalia's persistence, boldness, and faith?

Jesus was working something in Thalia as well. Drawing her in, gauging her hunger. Jim Cymbala describes his experience with Jesus taking him deeper. "I already knew, but God was now drawing me out, pulling me toward an actual experience of himself and his power. He was telling me that my hunger for him and his transforming power would be satisfied as I led my tiny congregation to call out to him in prayer."[28]

Thalia is the second foreigner, outsider, outcast, to delight Jesus, to touch His heart with great faith. And like the centurion, she received both an answer to her request, and a commendation as well. Do we long for the joy of Jesus's affirmation, his commendation? Let's let our hunger for Him drive our persistent seeking of Him. Don't give up. He takes great pleasure in and rewards those who diligently seek Him! What did Thalia discover about Jesus that day? Thalia recognized Jesus's Messiahship and His mercy, which enabled her to approach Him with a humility-infused boldness. We'll look next at a man who recognized Jesus's goodness, grace, and love.

## An Enthusiastic Seeker

Zacchaeus was a man who went to great measures to seek Jesus. Although a tax collector and probably more despised than even this Canaanite woman, he found Jesus, or rather Jesus found him. And the respectable onlookers were offended! His story and what he discovered about Jesus is next.

> *What man of you, having a hundred sheep, if he has lost one of them, does not leave the ninety-nine in the open country, and go after the one that is lost, until he finds it? —Jesus*
>
> —Luke 15:4

I bless you, dear, beloved, curious one,
To have your curiosity satisfied,
But more, to encounter Jesus in a transforming way,
And in this encounter,
To discover the true purpose of your life,
To experience the joy of Jesus's commendation
Of your change of heart leading to action.
And I bless you to discover,
That in your seeking of Jesus,
He has been seeking you!

# Chapter 7

## A Seeking Faith

*You have said, "Seek my face." My heart says to you,
"Your face, Lord, do I seek."*

—Psalm 27:8

Zacchaeus could hardly believe his luck. Jesus was coming through Jericho. This did not surprise him. Zacchaeus knew if Jesus were to travel to Jerusalem for the Passover, He would come this way, by the Jericho Road. A little longer perhaps, but if one wanted to avoid Samaria, with a populace as hostile to the Jews as was the mountainous terrain, this was the way to come. Though Zacchaeus could not be sure Jesus would come, he knew he was in the right place if He did. Now the gathering crowds offered confirmation. Jesus was on the way, and if Zacchaeus were ever to find out who this Jesus was, it would have to be now.

So, he pressed into the crowd as far as he could, hoping to get a glimpse, and as Jesus approached, he saw nothing. Zacchaeus jumped up and down, but it was no use. He was short of stature, and the crowds were great. To see anything, he would have to get ahead of them somehow.

Zacchaeus looked down the road where the crowds had not yet swelled, gathered his cloak, and ran. He wondered briefly how undignified this might look for a man in his position. Zacchaeus was rich. And not just rich but wealthy. He was the chief tax collector for the region, and as distasteful as his occupation was to his fellow Jews, he still had many friends. His money, and the parties it paid for, guaranteed that. Yes, his was a good life, and yet, there was something...

The sight of a tree ahead interrupted his thoughts. It was close to the road, and massive. *Just perfect*, he thought as he grabbed a limb and began to climb, the smaller branches tickling his face as a mother might tickle a child. He chuckled. If he looked undignified running, imagine what people would think now as he climbed hand over hand, like a common *yeled*, child!

Zacchaeus settled in a crook and waited, resuming his reverie. What was it about this Jesus that aroused his curiosity? And if his life was so good, what was it he sought? The crowd began to gather under the tree, and suddenly there He was, but not how Zacchaeus had imagined. This was no regal figure adorned with expensive clothes, surrounded with an aloof air of self-importance. Jesus dressed simply. A plain cloth tunic accented by a simple red woolen cloak stood in stark contrast to the multicolored garments of linen and fine wool worn by Zacchaeus. And Jesus conversed with those in the crowd, smiling, His eyes and hands speaking words punctuating those from His lips. Zacchaeus gaped as he leaned forward to get a better view. Jesus stopped, craned his neck, and looked at him, catching his open-mouthed, wide-eyed gaze. "Zacchaeus, hurry up, come down from there. I must stay at your house today!"

*He... He knows me?* Zacchaeus scrambled to the ground. If Zacchaeus was shocked at this, those looking on were more so. As he joyfully received Jesus, his reaction only highlighted the disappointment of the crowd.

"Why, He has gone to be the guest of a man who is a sinner!" many grumbled in amazement as Jesus walked with Zacchaeus toward his house, His arm around his shoulders.

The rest of that day would linger in Zacchaeus's memory like the sweet fragrance of a cut rose remembered long after its blossoms withered. He had sent a servant on ahead to arrange fresh water to wash Jesus's feet, a lavish meal to be prepared, and friends, sinners though they were, to invite. The hours of conversation, first privately, then continuing into supper with his guests as Jesus talked about His Father's Kingdom, the Kingdom of Heaven, had touched something deep within Zacchaeus.

And he had responded. Like the light from a freshly lit lamp illuminates a room previously shrouded in darkness, the purpose of his life, his wealth, suddenly clarified. As an old wineskin cannot contain the dynamic fermentation of new wine, neither could Zacchaeus contain this newfound joy as he leapt to his feet. "Behold, Lord," he said. "The half of my goods I give to the poor. And if I have defrauded anyone of anything, I restore it fourfold!"

Zacchaeus would never forget Jesus's response, nor the blazing flame of His eyes as He pronounced a commendation. "Today, salvation has come to this house since he also is a son of Abraham! For the Son of Man came to seek and to save the lost."

Zacchaeus now knew he had been lost. But he did not know at the time that this would be Jesus's final journey to Jerusalem, that those who initially received Him with joy as He entered the city would turn against him within a week and demand His death. That this rose would be cut from the vine, its petals torn from its stem as it was nailed to a cross in a painful death to pay for Zacchaeus's sin.

Yet the sweet fragrance remained. And in three days it grew more intense as Zacchaeus heard reports of the impossible, of Jesus's resurrection, this buried stem, this branch of Jesse, bursting forth in the new life and glorious radiance of full blossom. And Zacchaeus kept his promise as new life burst forth in him as well.[k]

## Jesus Commends Those Who Seek Him Enthusiastically

Zacchaeus was curious. You may be as well. He did not seek Jesus, as did Thalia, with a desperation-fueled boldness. In fact, he didn't feel a need for Him at all. It's just that he had heard much about Him, and, well, inquisitive minds want to know. So, Zacchaeus pursued Jesus enthusiastically. His was not a half-hearted quest. The risk of public humiliation, loss of dignity, and the possibility of damage to his expensive garments—none of these deterred him. Jesus took great delight in this pursuit. Can you just picture the amusement on Jesus's face as He caught Zacchaeus's attention up in the tree?

What did Zacchaeus discover about Jesus that day that satisfied his curiosity? He saw Jesus's moral purity but also discovered Him as approachable. Although Jesus is holier than all, He did not portray Himself as holier than thou. Don't miss the divine paradox here. Although Jesus was sinless, He attracted rather than repulsed sinners. Those who the respectable in society ostracized were drawn to Jesus.

---

[k] The story of Zacchaeus and some of the dialogue is taken from Luke 19:1–10.

We have all, most likely, heard of Jesus and have formed an opinion of Him based on what we have heard. I grew up going to church. I learned Mary, a virgin, gave birth to the infant Jesus. He was the Son of God, lived a perfect life, was executed on a Roman cross, and three days later, rose from the dead. And then, I ignored Him. I quit church during my sophomore year of high school.

Our experience of Jesus has little to do with what we have learned or been taught of Him. It has everything to do with what we do with Him. I knew far more of Jesus than did Zacchaeus. Yet he was determined, if only out of curiosity, to find out more. I don't know if Zacchaeus expected he would literally meet Jesus. But he did. And Jesus rewarded this curiosity-driven enthusiasm to see Him with much more than Zacchaeus expected. It would be two years after I quit church that my curiosity would be awakened, and I would meet Him as well.

What will we do with what we know of Jesus? Will we be satisfied with whatever opinion we have formed of Him, content to have answered one of life's questions now neatly tucked away for future reference, but with no immediate relevance to our lives? Or will we enthusiastically pursue Him, not knowing what to expect other than a desire for His life to impact ours?

## Jesus Commends Those Who Find Him and Receive Him Joyfully

At the risk of sounding obvious, there can be no finding without seeking. It has always been this way. The prophet Jeremiah sought to encourage the Judean exiles in Babylon with the following words, often clung to by those in difficult circumstance: "For I know the plans I have for you, declares the Lord, plans for welfare and not for evil, to give you a future and a hope" (Jeremiah 29:11).

What follows is often bypassed yet holds even greater significance. "Then you will call upon me and come and pray to me, and I will hear you. You will seek me and find me, when you seek me with all your heart" (Jeremiah 29:12–13).

Jesus, when teaching his followers how to pray, encouraged them to keep asking, seeking, and knocking.[1] God takes great delight in our pursuit of Him, and the more enthusiasm, the greater His pleasure. But it is the Father who awakens this curiosity of Jesus. Jesus initiates our pursuit of Him. Listen to Jesus's words: "No one can come to me unless the Father who sent me draws him. And I will raise him up on the last day" (John 6:44).

Like discovering our first crush also has a crush on us, we experience great joy when we realize Jesus has been dying to reveal himself to us. More on this in a moment. Brennan Manning observes, "Uncontaminated trust in the revelation of Jesus allows us to breathe more freely, to dance more joyfully, and to sing more gratefully about the gift of salvation."[29]

Zacchaeus must have been astounded when Jesus caught his gaze, far up in the tree. He thought he was seeking Jesus only to discover Jesus was pursuing him. And he responded with great joy, throwing a party in Jesus's honor. A joy which gave Jesus great pleasure and which He commended.

## Jesus Commends Those Who Repent

There is a progression here. Jesus seeks us and puts a desire on our hearts to seek Him. When we seek Him with all our hearts, we will find Him. When we find Him, we discover joy. And we

---

[1] "And I tell you, ask, and it will be given to you; seek, and you will find; knock, and it will be opened to you. For everyone who asks receives, and the one who seeks finds, and to the one who knocks it will be opened" (Luke 11:9–10).

then value Him more than anything else. The extent of our joy depends on the extent to which we value Jesus and allow Him to lead us in repentance. And when joy fills us, it will overflow in our desire to bring joy and blessing to others.

Repentance is a natural result of an encounter with Jesus. When He reveals Himself, we see Him as He truly is and grasp the significance of what He has done. And repentance transforms us. It leads to a God-enabled change of both attitude and action. For Zacchaeus, it was a commitment to not only reform his tax collection practices but to also make restitution to those he had defrauded. This was a commitment that Jesus commended in His pronouncement of salvation.

The moment came similarly, and differently, for me. Fast-forward to the beginning of my senior year in high school. Like Zacchaeus, I felt no need for Jesus in the moment. Unlike Zacchaeus, I was not actively seeking Him. But He was seeking me. Although I knew much that was accurate about Jesus, I had not yet met Him. And there was one critical piece of information about Him, and about me, that I had missed.

My parents were out of town, and I had been invited to spend the night at a young couple's home. After dinner, we retired to the living room where they shared their story of how they had met Jesus and how He had healed their failing marriage. They also filled the gaps in my theological knowledge! Using a pamphlet, *The Four Spiritual Laws*,[m] they explained God's love for me, why I had not yet met Him, and what I was missing.

I wrote earlier, "Jesus has been dying to reveal himself to us." I learned that God's holiness, and my sinfulness, like fire and water,

---

[m] http://www.4laws.com/laws/englishkgp/default.htm

cannot coexist. Flavius recognized this when he declared himself unworthy of Jesus's visit. There is a deep chasm between me and God, and that chasm is my sin. If God is holy, that sin has to be judged. Like a platoon leader who falls on a hand grenade to save the lives of his troops, there must be a hero to bear the judgment I deserve so that I might be saved. One must sacrifice his life to atone for my sin. Although I had never previously thought of myself as a sinner, coming face to face with the holiness of Jesus, the meaning of his death, and the fact that I did not know God personally, starkly revealed my condition. My self-centeredness, anger, lies, my amusement in making fun of others—all of this painted an ugly picture. Jesus offered to be that hero. It was an offer I couldn't refuse. That evening I prayed to receive God's offer of forgiveness, to acknowledge Jesus's sacrifice for my sin, and to receive Him as Lord.

I woke the next morning to a beautiful fall day with a changed heart. I noticed two things immediately as I stepped outside. First, it was as if I had been seeing the world in black and white, and as one who has upgraded their television, I now saw it in Technicolor (we didn't have UHD 4K back then)! Second, the desire to swear, something I would do often, with or without cause, left. And now I began to seek. I wanted to learn as much as I could about this Jesus who had just revealed His mercy to me.

Repentance is God-initiated and God-enabled. It begins with a revelation from Him, who He is, His character, nature, and holiness which creates a change of heart. But repentance is incomplete without a change of action, a change that God must enable. And this enablement comes from the Holy Spirit. There is much about God's Holy Spirit, the third person of the triune God, in the Bible. He is referred to as the Comforter, counselor, revealer of Christ, and sanctifier. He is also a gift, the Promise of the Father, who indwells those who receive Christ.[n]

As we continue to follow the roadmap God has given us, the road now forks. We have taken the on-ramp of understanding God's design for us is for His pleasure in relationship with Him. We progress to the destination of the fullness of joy in His affirmation and commendation, not based on our performance but on what Jesus has done for us on the cross. Jesus has another word for this destination, Eternal Life, knowing Him and the Father.[o] And, we learn how to return His love, what brings Him pleasure, as we go.

There is now, before us, a large green sign with a big white arrow pointing straight ahead. Under the arrow, words direct: "To God's Affirmation, Joy City, follow HR Repentance." We quickly realize this is not an interstate, that HR refers to Heaven's Route. But there is also an exit sign off to our right bearing the words "Complacency Cove," with a white arrow pointing the way.

We can get off here. We do not have to take the repentance route. It is like the blue pill/red pill offered to the oblivious Neo in the movie *The Matrix*. We can exit now, avoiding the discomforting reality of who we are, and live in ignorant, though mundane, faux bliss. Or we can take the red pill, the repentance road of facing the unpleasant truth about ourselves but arriving at the joyful reality of God's unconditional love and affirmation. If we exit, we will never discover the reality of our true identity, and

---

[n] Peter promises the Holy Spirit to those who believe. "And Peter said to them, 'Repent and be baptized every one of you in the name of Jesus Christ for the forgiveness of your sins, and you will receive the gift of the Holy Spirit'" (Acts 2:38). Jesus elaborates on His promise of the Holy Spirit during His last meal with His disciples in John 16:5–15.

[o] "And this is eternal life, that they know you, the only true God, and Jesus Christ whom you have sent" (John 17:3).

acceptance offered by Jesus in relationship with the Father. We will never experience eternal life. Zacchaeus took the red pill. He allowed Jesus's holiness to expose his greed and corruption and experienced the joy of repentance and Jesus's forgiveness and commendation.

I hope you will continue the journey with me. Because we will meet one of Jesus's disciples, an impulsive man, one who would deny he ever knew Jesus, but one to whom the Father revealed Jesus, who recognized Jesus's greatest quality, and who brought Jesus great joy because he got it!

*But blessed are your eyes, for they see, and your ears, for they hear.* —*Jesus*

—Matthew 13:16

I bless you, beloved child of God,

With the awakening of your spiritual eyes,

To see Jesus in a new way,

A fresh revelation from the Father,

To get an exponentially greater view,

Of who He is,

I bless you when you revert to seeing Jesus,

Through human eyes,

To receive His gentle rebuke,

And I bless you to experience the full joy,

Of His gracious restoration,

And pleasure.

## Chapter 8

# A Great Confession of Faith

*In that same hour he rejoiced in the Holy Spirit and said,
"I thank you, Father, Lord of heaven and earth, that you
have hidden these things from the wise and understanding and revealed them to little children; yes, Father, for
such was your gracious will." —Jesus*

—Luke 10:21

*Is this a test?* Peter's guard was raised as soon as the question rolled off Jesus's lips.

"Who do people say that the Son of Man is?" Jesus had asked. Peter bit his tongue. Not that he was shy or at a loss for words. He always had an opinion and was quick to voice it. It's just that he had been burned before. Some of Jesus's questions simply didn't make sense, which Peter once pointed out. They had all been walking together, surrounded by a throng of the curious. Jesus asked the crowd pressing in against Him who had touched Him.

"How can you ask who touched you?" Peter had said. "Everyone is touching you!" And then he had been quite awed, if not a little embarrassed, to discover that a woman with a chronic hemorrhage had been healed… just by touching the hem of Jesus's robe. So now he kept silent. He would let others make fools of themselves while he looked on. He would not risk having another bad day.

"Some say you are John the Baptist," exclaimed one of the disciples.

*That's the stupidest thing I've ever heard.* Peter smiled and congratulated himself on his newfound restraint. He listened quietly as the responses continued.

"Others say you are Elijah."

"There are some who say you are Jeremiah… or another prophet," another offered.

But even as he sat quietly, something began to build inside Peter. Something he couldn't quite explain. It was not the urgency of a boiling pot of water ready to overflow. It was more like a dawning realization. Even as the rising sun gradually illuminates a landscape bound and veiled in darkness and sets it free, revealing it in a moment of blazing light, so Peter saw in Jesus something previously hidden. He had already come to believe that Jesus was the Messiah, the hope and redeemer of Israel, but now, as he looked at Him, there was something else, something much greater, something that was full of glory.

As if on cue came Jesus's next question, "But who do you say that I am?"

Peter spoke, but not with the exuberance of a young student who has the right answer to his teacher's question. He spoke rather as one who has suddenly discovered an obvious answer to a perplexing problem and wonders why he has not seen it before. "You are the Christ, the Son of the living God."

Jesus turned toward Peter, eyes dancing and grin widening, pleased not only by the answer but as much so by who offered it.

"Blessed are you, Simon Bar-Jonah! For flesh and blood has not revealed this to you, but my Father who is in heaven. And I tell you, you are Peter, and on this rock I will build my church, and the gates of hell shall not prevail against it. I will give you the keys of the kingdom of heaven, and whatever you bind on earth shall be bound in heaven, and whatever you loose on earth shall be loosed in heaven."[p]

## God Commends Those Who Receive His Revelation of His Son

Jesus commends those who receive revelation from the Father. But this is not a "good for you" commendation, as if we had something to do with it. As with Zacchaeus, and my own encounter with Jesus, it is God who takes the initiative to reveal. We cannot figure out who He is on our own. God must awaken something dead in us to perceive spiritual reality. And He does this through the Holy Spirit. Jesus describes this awakening as being born again. And He likens the Holy Spirit to the wind. Consider His encounter with Nicodemus.

Nicodemus was not just any Pharisee. He was one of the most revered, a ruler, a person of respect. He was also disillusioned. He had spent years studying, achieving expertise in the law. Yet he realized something deeper was missing. Some of his students discouraged him, zealously pursuing the legalistic requirements of the law, ignoring its intent. And this disillusionment led him to seek a meeting with Jesus. He would only meet Him at night, though; he had a reputation to protect, after all. Still, he recognized God had to be with Jesus, so he went, seeking

---

[p] The story of Peter's confession of Christ and some of the included is paraphrased from Matthew 16:13–20.

to understand the truth, the something more, of God's Kingdom. And Jesus engaged him.

"Truly, truly, I say to you, unless one is born again he cannot see the kingdom of God."[30]

Nicodemus shrugged, his arms outstretched. "How can a man be born when he is old? Can he enter a second time into his mother's womb and be born?"[31]

Jesus answered, "Do not marvel that I said to you, 'You must be born again.' The wind blows where it wishes, and you hear its sound, but you do not know where it comes from or where it goes. So it is with everyone who is born of the Spirit" (John 3:7–8).

Jesus continued, explaining the truth of God's Kingdom, who He was, and why He came. "No one has ascended into heaven except he who descended from heaven, the Son of Man. And as Moses lifted up the serpent in the wilderness, so must the Son of Man be lifted up, that whoever believes in him may have eternal life. For God so loved the world, that he gave his only Son, that whoever believes in him should not perish but have eternal life. For God did not send His Son into the world to condemn the world, but in order that the world might be saved through him" (John 3:13–17).

Nicodemus left perplexed. But something had touched his heart. He would later defend Jesus before the Sanhedrin. He would also bring seventy-five pounds of spices to prepare Jesus's body for burial. When God reveals himself, He does not do so with proof. He reveals Himself with a conviction we must receive by faith.

## God Commends Those Who See with New Eyes

When God reveals Himself, He often enables us to see with new eyes, from a new perspective, in a way we haven't seen before. It is usually not a word-for-word message. Like standing at the rim of the Grand Canyon, taking in its grandeur up close and personal, when having previously only viewed it from thirty thousand feet, we see the same thing from an unfamiliar perspective. We experience great joy and awe in this new picture, one that instantly writes a tome upon our hearts, yet we struggle to describe it in words.

What did Peter discover about Jesus that day? He had been remarkably familiar with Jesus, knowing Him personally, and recognizing Him as the Messiah, the deliverer of Israel. But this new revelation was far greater. Peter now saw Jesus's divinity, His identity as the Son of God. And it changed everything.

Likewise, my view of Jesus changed when I recognized the meaning of the cross. As I acted on this revelation, receiving Him, a fresh view of everything opened around me, creating joy and awe. I was drawn back to church. Incredibly the meaning of Jesus's atoning sacrifice on the cross jumped off the pages of all the songs and liturgy and smacked me in the face as if to say, "Why did you not see this before?" The best way to answer is from the hymn *Amazing Grace.* "I once was blind but now I see." I had new eyes.

## Jesus Commends Those Who Receive the Father's Revelation and Reveals More

Jesus recognized the extraordinary blessing Peter had received from the Father. And He revealed more. The more included a promise. Peter would be foundational to the new church Jesus would build.[q] A great revelation from God carries with it a great

---

[q] Peter would emerge as the leader of those who gathered in the upper room for ten days of prayer as recorded in Acts 1. After the Holy Spirit fell on those gathered, Peter would preach a message resulting in the formation of this new church of about three thousand as recorded in Acts 2.

responsibility. It requires a deep trust to obey what comes next. It also requires a deep humility, realizing we have received part of a picture but there is much more we do not yet perceive. It is not about us. Receiving a revelation from God does not mean that we immediately understand all of His ways. But as we respond to what He reveals, what He allows us to know of Him, He reveals more of Himself.

Let's not miss the promise Jesus made. Even though Peter would be central in Jesus's church, he would not be the one to lead or build it. Jesus would. The promise came with a great responsibility but also with a great enabling.

## Jesus Restores Those He Commends

Though Peter had received a great revelation, he had much left to learn. In amazement, we note that Peter, having just recognized Jesus's divinity, rebukes Him when Jesus predicts His crucifixion. And Jesus addresses Peter as Satan![r] Yet Peter's impetuous blundering did not alter the Father's grace toward him, nor did it alter the purpose He would fulfill in Peter's life. God does not give up on us when we take the wrong path. He pursues us, restores us, and fulfills the promise He made to us. We may mess up; in fact, we will. But for those who receive, more will be revealed. Jesus restores those He commends.

God does not give up on us, even if we give up on Him. Can we internalize this fact? Make it our own? Hold on to it and not let go? This is where faith that leads to an act of trust results in hope. And hope is what keeps us going, especially amid suffering

---

[r] "But he turned and said to Peter, 'Get behind me, Satan! You are a hindrance to me. For you are not setting your mind on the things of God, but on the things of man'" (Matthew 16:23).

and trials. Hope can keep us from giving up and can draw us back to God if we do. And our hope in God brings Jesus great joy which He commends. Join me as we look at hope next and see what I discovered about Jesus as Kathy and I faced one of the biggest trials in our marriage.

*May the God of hope fill you with all joy and peace in believing, so that by the power of the Holy Spirit you may abound in hope.*

—Romans 15:13

I bless you, beloved child of God,
With the Father's gift of hope,
A hope that perseveres when trials loom,
A perseverance which trusts in the love and care of
God,
When circumstances scream otherwise,
And I bless you with the joy of His Presence,
And His pleasure,
As you grow to maturity,
And see His best for you unfold.

# Section 3

··•✦•··

# Hope

# Chapter 9

## Hope: It Keeps Us Moving

*And we desire each one of you to show the same*
*earnestness to have the full assurance of hope until the end.*

—Hebrews 6:11

If faith is that belief in the One unseen that causes us to act, hope is the trust in the object of our faith that keeps us from giving up. It is not a stubborn act of will. It is that firm belief that the One in whom we trust will not let us down, has our back, and will bring us to His desired outcome. Notice I didn't say it would bring us to our goal. Hope is not about us. It is the quality that believes that as we keep moving forward, God will accomplish His purpose. And we believe His purpose is for our good, for our best. Hope plays the role of developing maturity in our lives when we allow it to lead us.

## Hope Is the Vibrancy of Life

Trust is faith flowering, the beautiful blossom of the action step of faith. Hope is the ongoing vibrancy displayed long after the blossom fades. It withstands cold, heat, and drought, and it grows to maturity.

A large Bradford pear adorns our front yard. I love springtime when it is in full bloom. The myriad white blossoms make a stunning display as they intervene between the lush green grass and the azure blue sky, commanding attention as if to say, "Look at me!" The blossoms, however, are short-lived, scattered easily by a strong wind or unexpected frost. Yet the tree stands tenaciously in full leaf, withstanding the insolent heat of summer. It remains vibrant, despite its faded spring beauty, enduring even the dormancy of winter to blossom again at the appointed time. Such is the character of hope. It is easy to celebrate the rewards of faith when they appear quickly, such as in our move to Atlanta. It is quite something else to celebrate God, the object of our faith, when answers delay.

It was the fall of 1991, and I was teaching an adult Sunday School class on faith. Not able to conceive, we had sought adoption, having already experienced one heartbreak as a previous effort collapsed when the birth mother changed her mind. However, now our prayers were answered as we were selected to adopt a child due at Christmas. We shared the celebratory news with the class.

The most effective teaching comes from life experience, not just knowledge. If God calls you to teach, He will allow you to live the lesson He asks you to share. The new adoption fell through again as the birth mother changed her mind at birth. Although best for the child as the father committed to the birth mother and to the newborn, it devastated us. Kathy and I wordlessly dismantled the prepared nursery and returned the borrowed crib.

Our joy does not depend on our circumstances but on God, the object of our faith. Hope does not focus on the desired outcome but on the character of the One who has made the promise, and on the assurance that He will accomplish His purposes in and for us. This was the lesson I shared with our class. And Sherri, a member of our class, tore up a note on which she had written a message she received from God.

## Hope Keeps Us Going

It was early 1992 when the young boy squared to the foul line, eyes set on the rim, elbow and forearm aligned with the basket. His father spoke encouragement. "You can do it. Focus. Don't give up!" Thomas was discouraged. He had missed his two previous free throws, and this was his last shot. In one smooth motion, Thomas elevated his elbow, flicked his wrist, and released the ball. It arced toward the rim and swished. Nothing but net! Everyone cheered!

However, this was not a basketball game. It was a children's sermon staged on the church platform with a plastic backboard and toy ball. The message, "If you have a Godly goal, don't give up, keep trying, persevere!" seemed aimed squarely at me. Over the next two months, I wrote letters to unwed mothers' ministries, addressed toward potential birth mothers. One of these letters, at one of these homes, was picked from a stack. We were chosen to adopt! We met the birth mother in the hospital shortly after she delivered on October 1, 1992, and she offered her child, our son Daniel, to us. Oh, and the message from God Sherri had received in October of 1991, written down, and then torn up? She told us later. "David and Kathy will have a child by this time next year!"

## Hope Builds Maturity

*Count it all joy, my brothers, when you meet trials of various kinds, for you know that the testing of your faith produces steadfastness. And let steadfastness have its full effect, that you may be perfect and complete, lacking in nothing.*

—James 1:2–4

We encounter trials because we exist in a world broken by sin and rebellion. How we respond to these trials determines the extent to which we please Jesus. Listen to the words of the author of Hebrews as he discusses faith: "But my righteous one shall live by faith, and if he shrinks back, my soul has no pleasure in him" (Hebrews 10:38).

Do you want to experience the joy of the Father's pleasure, even in ongoing trials? Brennan Manning writes of the joy the Father takes in trust-infused hope: "Trust is that rare and priceless treasure that wins us the affection of our heavenly Father."[32]

How we respond to trials also determines the extent to which we grow and mature. Do we receive correction with humility when the trials are of our own making? Do we respond with the steadfastness of hope and developing Christian character when they are not? Trials teach. Kathy and I sought counseling from our associate pastor to deal with the pain of our disappointment and our lashing out at each other. We learned how to treat each other's pain gently. Kathy learned to release her desire for a child to the Father in pleasing trust. I learned to take her desire seriously and take initiative as I approached maternity ministries with perseverance. What did we discover about Jesus? He is steadfast to sustain us during difficult days. He brings joy as we trust in times of trouble. And our patience in hope provides Him great pleasure.

How do we develop such hope that enables us to persevere in trials? Brennan Manning writes, "Faith arises from the personal experience of Jesus as Lord. Hope is reliance on the promise of Jesus, accompanied by the expectation of fulfillment. Trust is the winsome wedding of faith and hope."[33]

When we encounter Jesus, see Him as He truly is, experience His love, submit gratefully to Him as Lord, we increasingly trust Him. We also receive the enabling gift of the Holy Spirit. What does the response to trials look like which pleases Jesus, which He commends? The Apostle Paul describes this to the Galatian Church: "But the fruit of the Spirit is love, joy, peace, patience, kindness, goodness, faithfulness, gentleness, self-control" (Galatians 5:22–23a).

We will look next at those who persevered through obstacles and trials to reach Jesus—a perseverance of faith which He rewarded and commended. Consider now a desperate woman with a chronic illness, who pushed through crowds to reach Jesus and would not give up until she touched Him. Let's see what she discovered about Jesus that met not only her physical needs but much more.

*And forgive us our debts, as we also have forgiven our debtors.*

—Matthew 6:12

I bless you, beloved child of God,
To take your brokenness to Jesus,
To push through,

To not give up,
I bless you to receive more than you ask,
As you persevere,
I bless you with the joy,
Of Jesus's commendation and healing,
As you give and receive forgiveness,
And I bless you with the joy,
Of reconciliation to God and others.

# Chapter 10

## Her Last Resort

*Daughter, your faith has made you well; go in peace, and
be healed of your disease. —Jesus*

—Mark 5:34

*E*liana's world seemed an atrocious absurdity. What had once
been a promising life lay in ruins. Her beauty, health, friends,
and money were gone. All stolen by a relentless physical bleeding that had systematically taken everything away from her like
a thief in the night who returns day after day over a twelve-year
period, until there is nothing left to take.

The rabbis had not helped. With hope and expectancy, she
had performed the dictated washing rituals. When she returned
to them after the prescribed eighty days, still bleeding, they
declared her officially and permanently unclean. Now ostracized,
she could never again join worshippers in the synagogue on Sabbath days. The rabbis even required her to celebrate the Passover
privately, a month after everyone else…alone!

The only people who would associate with her were the
physicians whom she had sought in desperation. *The physicians.*

Eliana's face pinched. *Little help they were.* And now that all her money was gone, they would no longer treat her. Eliana had given up seeking the unanswered why. It no longer mattered. And now, like a beaten puppy cowers and hides before its abuser, Eliana shrunk back, hiding from life, believing this was all she deserved, all she would ever receive. So, she isolated to avoid further blows.

Yet, one day something invaded her darkness. Like the first cry of a rooster penetrating the dark veil of sleep, the clamoring of the crowd outside her house roused Eliana from her ruminations and sparked a curiosity which drew her into the street. It was there she saw Him.

Eliana recognized the young rabbi at the center of the throng, conversing warmly with those around Him. Jesus had taken up residence in Capernaum, her hometown, the previous year. She had not only heard the stories, but she had seen the healings. A centurion's servant, a paralytic, and others, now walking around, alive and healthy. Even the despised local tax collector, Matthew, had left his booth and followed Jesus.

Eliana had considered going to Him. Yet her experience with the other rabbis and the potential rejection from her official impure status had dissuaded her. So, she continued to expend her resources on physicians.

But she discovered something extraordinary as she listened. Reports from Decapolis recounted how Jesus had just transformed the violent, possessed "demoniac of Gadara" into a man now completely sane. Could it be that this possessed man, who had lived naked among the tombs, breaking chains and thwarting every attempt to bind him, was now whole and in his right mind?[s]

---

[s] The story of the Gerasene demoniac is found in Mark 5:1–20.

*Well, if Jesus will heal such a defiled man, might He be willing?*
A man determinedly pushing his way through the crowd interrupted Eliana's thoughts. She recognized him as well. Jairus.
He was one of the synagogue rulers who had pronounced her
unclean. She seethed as she remembered the day.

Yet he did not approach Jesus as the self-assured, authori-
tarian figure she knew. Improbably, an air of desperation, even
humility, surrounded him. Then Eliana gasped as Jairus did the
unthinkable, throwing himself prostrate on the ground at Jesus's
feet. He cried out, "My little daughter is at the point of death.
Come and lay your hands on her, so that she may be made well
and live."

Eliana gaped as Jesus grasped Jairus's hand, pulled him to his
feet, and immediately began to go with him. A swell of emotions
washed over Eliana, battering her as storm waves from the Sea
of Galilee batter the shore. The old, buried resentment toward
the synagogue rulers burst uncontrollably to the surface as she
watched her opportunity slipping away, robbed once again by him
who had declared her contaminated.

Then unexpectedly, a new emotion arose, displacing her icy
resentment as a warm fire overpowers the chill of a room on a
frosty day. Eliana experienced a growing compassion toward
Jairus. She would not barge in and interrupt. As one unclean,
she doubted this young rabbi would respond. She wasn't allowed
to touch Him. But perhaps...perhaps if she could just get close
enough, maybe if she could just touch Jesus's robe.

Eliana shrouded her head and weaved through the following crowd. She would remain as invisible as possible as she
approached Jesus from behind. She reached between two of His
disciples, her fingers briefly caressing the bottom of His garment.
And as she withdrew her hand, preparing to disappear back into

the crowd, it happened. An intense tingling flowed through her body, traveling up her arm, radiating through her chest, upward, downward, and outward through her other arm, infusing her with a newfound vitality.

But there was more. A pervasive sense of love, peace, and joy enveloped her as a mother's arms might swaddle an infant. Instantly, she knew she was healed, not just physically, but she was now whole, clean, and pure, in every sense of the word.

Eliana's peace was short-lived, broken by an authoritative voice that rang out above the noisy crowd. "Who touched me?" asked Jesus as He stopped and scanned those around Him. She hid in terror as one by one, those around Jesus proclaimed their innocence.

"Master, how can you ask, 'Who touched me?'" declared one of Jesus's disciples, clearly perturbed at this delay of such an urgent mission. "Everyone is touching you!"

"No, no," Jesus replied, continuing to slowly survey the crowd. "Someone touched me. I felt power go out from me."

Eliana glanced at Jairus, then Jesus, then back at Jairus, who was clearly distressed at the apparent interruption of Jesus's ministry to his daughter. She moved toward Jesus, trembling as Jairus looked on with shocked recognition. She fell face down at Jesus's feet, loudly declaring all she had done and the healing she received. Jesus warmed Eliana with His eyes as He raised her up. "Daughter, your faith has made you well; go in peace, and be healed of your disease."

Time stopped for Eliana. Now her trembling was not out of fear but in awe of Him. Her only desire was to remain in the presence of this One who cared, who loved, who set her free. A freedom not only from the physical ravages of her ailment but from the deeper, tormenting anger, fear, despair, and loneliness she had endured.

A new voice broke through her wonder. One of Jairus's household approached solemnly. "Sir, your daughter is dead." He reached out, laying his hand on Jairus's shoulder, and looked sympathetically into his eyes. "Why trouble the Teacher any further?"

Jairus's eyes flooded as he turned toward Eliana, who could only look back apologetically as banished feelings of unworthiness clawed back to the surface. They stared at each other for what seemed like minutes. Jesus interrupted. "Do not fear; only believe."

Jesus beckoned to Peter, James, and his brother John to accompany Him as He proceeded with Jairus toward his house, motioning to the others to remain behind. Eliana reluctantly complied. Eager for any news of Jesus, she soon learned of another miracle in Capernaum. Jesus had raised Jairus's daughter to life!ᵗ

It was now the next Sabbath, and Eliana, with great anticipation, approached the synagogue for the first time in twelve years. As she drew near, she saw Jairus holding his daughter's hand, expectantly searching the crowd. As their eyes met, two large men in long, ornate robes blocked her view. Eliana recognized them as Pharisees by their dress. With stern looks and arms crossed, they blocked her way. *Did Jairus send them?* She stiffened.

The men approached, when suddenly Eliana saw them jerked backward by two strong arms. She heard a loud voice saying, "Stand aside and let her enter, you fools." She recognized the voice. Jairus! As the befuddled Pharisees looked on, Jairus took

---

ᵗ The story of a hemorrhagic woman and Jairus, including some of the paraphrased dialogue, is found in Mark 5:21–43. The story of Eliana meeting Jairus and his daughter at the temple is not part of the biblical text.

one of Eliana's hands and his daughter took the other. "Come in, come in!" said Jairus. "Welcome, daughter of God!"

Eliana and Jairus exchanged knowing looks as they ascended the stairs together. Looks that, although unnoticed by others, expressed a mixture of forgiveness, joy, and wonder. Their worship would come alive this morning as they shared an awe of the young rabbi whose miraculous, redemptive work exceeded the mere physical.

## Jesus Commends Those Who Persevere to Reach Him

The lines between faith and hope overlap. Jesus commends those who push through in faith, and it is the perseverance in hope which gives legs to that faith. Eliana did not possess the boldness of the Canaanite woman who audaciously harried Jesus in the face of His apparent indifference. In fact, Eliana was quite timid, beat down, and hoped to receive what she needed unnoticed. Jesus had not even been her first choice. As a gambler doubles down on his losses, hoping his luck will change, Eliana had stuck with the physicians until all her resources were depleted. But she came to believe in Jesus's power. And this spark of faith propelled her toward Jesus, even at the risk of discovery by Jairus.

## Jesus Rewards Perseverance with More than We Expect

What did Eliana discover about Jesus that day? Eliana found that His power was greater than just a physical restoration. Jesus made her whole in every way. Jesus gives more than we expect. We may not even know what to expect, but faith-fueled hope trusts that Jesus will give us what we need.

It doesn't matter if you do not seek Jesus first. We often turn to Him only in desperation, after all else has failed. This is of no consequence. When we do turn to Him, we respond to the Father's initiative, His invitation. Have we ignored Jesus, seeking to face life's problems with our own resources? Are we afraid we have offended Jesus and are too embarrassed to turn to Him? Don't hold back. We can bring our needs to Him, regardless of the past. He gives generously without reproach.[u] Our turning pleases Him greatly. And you might be surprised to receive more than you expect.

## Jesus Commends Those Who Extend and Receive Forgiveness

*For if you forgive others their trespasses, your heavenly Father will also forgive you. —Jesus*

—Matthew 6:14

The hope of physical healing launched Eliana's journey toward Jesus. But in His touch, she found forgiveness, emotional healing, and a reborn spirit as well. Forgiveness can be a chicken-and-egg proposition. Do we forgive first, which allows God's forgiveness? Or does God forgive us first and then call us to extend that forgiveness to others? I would say the latter.

When we fully receive the forgiveness the Father offers, understanding the love-motivated cost Jesus paid, we cannot help but forgive others. Jesus emphasized this significance in His follow-up to His teaching on prayer. "For if you forgive others their trespasses, your heavenly Father will also forgive you, but if you do not forgive others their trespasses, neither will your

---

[u] "If any of you lacks wisdom, let him ask God, who gives generously to all without reproach, and it will be given him" (James 1:5).

Father forgive your trespasses" (Matthew 6:14–15). This is the only aspect of the Lord's Prayer on which He elaborated, just to make sure we get the point.

The biggest block to receiving healing is unforgiveness. As Eliana approached Jesus, her bitterness toward those who had abused her fell away. She even felt compassion for Jairus in his pain. As she grasped Jesus's garment, she grasped His love and forgiveness, allowing her to forgive others and receive all Jesus offered.

Forgiveness is not a natural human affection. It is a divine disposition. The only way we grant forgiveness is to receive it from God. As we draw closer to Jesus, like Eliana, it is unthinkable not to forgive. And as we forgive, we please Jesus immensely. Heaven opens and all that Jesus has for us pours down, including His approval and commendation.

## Jesus Cares for the Crushed

Jesus has a special affinity for the abused, care for the crushed, devotion to the distressed, and passion for the poor. He said so when describing His mission, a quote from the prophet Isaiah to a crowd in His hometown of Nazareth at the onset of His public ministry.

> *The Spirit of the Lord is upon me,*
> *because he has anointed me*
> *to proclaim good news to the poor.*
> *He has sent me to proclaim liberty to the captives*
> *and recovering of sight to the blind,*
> *to set at liberty those who are oppressed,*
> *to proclaim the year of the Lord's favor.*
> *—Jesus*

—Luke 4:18-19

Unhappily, this crowd consisted of respectable religious people in the local synagogue. They responded favorably at first, then tried to kill Jesus. His offense? He dared to address their sense of entitlement as special, deserving of the same miracles He had performed in Capernaum, a more multiethnic town. Jesus highlighted past acts of God's grace—healing and provision directed toward Gentiles at the exclusion of Israel.

Those who feel ostracized by religious people, on the fringes, unacceptable and unworthy, are precious to Jesus. They often see Him in a way that religious people don't. There is an interesting contrast here between Eliana and Jairus. One ostracized and beaten down, the other confident and powerful. But both desperate and seeking Jesus. Jesus does not discriminate. He gives both more than expected. He lavishes physical, emotional, and spiritual healing, forgiveness, and reconciliation, and raises the dead to new life! If we feel brokenhearted, disappointed in life, and ostracized, we are the very ones for whom Jesus came, searched, and gave His life. He offers us the joy of His pleasure as we seek Him.

Jesus came for another one ostracized as well, and for good reason. Lavan was a tax collector. Nobody likes tax collectors, but Lavan was a special kind of opportunist. Although a parable, this tale highlights the distinction between those who are self-righteous and those who are self-aware. Thus far, we have noticed humility as a significant characteristic that brings Jesus joy and receives His commendation. Here, Jesus laserfocuses on this quality, contrasts it with pride, and sets it as the foundational quality for justification with God. Let's hear this powerful parable next and see what Lavan discovers about God's mercy.

*He also told this parable to some who trusted in themselves
that they were righteous, and treated others with contempt:
"Two men went up into the temple to pray, one a Pharisee
and the other a tax collector."*

—Luke 18:9–10

I bless you, beloved of God,
With a spirit of humility,
I bless you to cease striving,
Having nothing to prove,
I bless you when you feel,
You have nothing to offer,
To encounter the joy of the Father's mercy,
And I bless you to receive,
His commendation of justification,
And the joy of the assurance,
Of right standing with Him.

# Chapter 11

# Justified by God

*Though the Lord is great, he cares for the humble, but he
keeps his distance from the proud.*

—Psalm 138:6 NLT

Lavan strode resolutely toward the temple, his desperation
strengthening his determination, and winning the debate
against his trepidation as an orator demolishing his opponent.
But Lavan was no orator. He was a tax collector and preferred to
let the official seal of the Roman proconsul do his talking. He had
won that stamp of authority by submitting the highest bid to the
Roman government. And he was able to collect enough above the
bid from his fellow Jews to make a tidy profit.

Lavan was not religious and normally would avoid the temple.
And why should he go? It's not that he didn't believe in the God
of Israel; it's just that he had already suffered enough contempt.
Respectable Jews shunned him, so why would he expose himself
to more humiliation? However, something had been bothering
Lavan recently. He could not avoid a growing awareness of his
defect of character. He could barely look in a mirror anymore and

would lower his eyes when he saw his own reflection. So, on this day, he went. His resolve to get right with God trumped his fear of public scorn.

But how would he get right with God? What could he possibly say or offer? Lavan pondered the possibilities. As he pondered, he concluded there was nothing, no quality of character to claim, and certainly no amount of money, confiscated as it was from his fellow man in the name of Rome that could make things right. The closer he got to the temple, the greater grew his sense of poverty. A sense of poverty that for a rich man such as himself was quite unsettling.

His steps slowed, but he was still drawn toward the temple, as if a giant unseen arm had him about the shoulders, compelling him forward, his feet and legs following in irresistible compliance. And now he was there. Lavan resolutely climbed the giant stairs leading to the double gate where pilgrims entered and made his way to the place of prayer. There he noticed a regal man in flowing robes, praying loudly, passersby directing admiring glances his way. Lavan drew closer. Perhaps he could learn something about prayer from this Pharisee.

The Pharisee stood. "I thank you, God, that I am not a sinner like everyone else. For I don't cheat, I don't sin, and I don't commit adultery." He glanced at Lavan. "I'm certainly not like that tax collector! I fast twice a week, and I give you a tenth of my income."[v]

*There is nothing in that prayer I can use.* Lavan walked away, distancing himself from the crowd as the Pharisee droned on,

---

[v] Jesus taught this parable to emphasize justification comes from humility and God's mercy, not performance, and is found in Luke 18:9–14. Some of the dialogue is paraphrased, and some of the content is not in the biblical text.

his sense of poverty overwhelming. He found a secluded corner and began to beat his chest. Slowly at first, then with increasing intensity until his fists numbed. His eyes cast to the ground, and flowing with tears, he wailed. "God, be merciful to me, a sinner."

As he cried out, a giant weight lifted, and simultaneously, a warmth grew inside him. A peace enveloped and softened him, and his cries of wailing turned to cries of gratitude. "Thank you, God! Thank you, God!"

Lavan turned to leave, inexplicably having received that for which he had come but knew he didn't deserve. He passed the Pharisee on the way, the gathering crowd still drawn to his eloquent prayer as flies to dung. Lavan didn't care. He felt clean for the first time. And his name, Lavan—meaning "white"—finally fit.

## Jesus Commends and Justifies the Humble

*The humble will be filled with fresh joy from the Lord. The poor will rejoice in the Holy One of Israel.*

—Isaiah 29:19 NLT

There is an uncluttered path to getting right with God. In many dramas, the hero is about to dispatch the villain and encourages him to get right with God. Theologians call this "justification." It refers to the state of being accepted by God, declared "not guilty." What would you do or say in those final moments of your life?

Would it surprise you to learn that the villain's humble cry for mercy would touch God more than the hero's claim to a righteous life? Humility attracts God. He commends and justifies the humble. The truly humble will seek justification from God, not from others. When we seek affirmation from others, we will feel either inadequate or superior in comparison, leaving an inaccurate sense of self.

What do you think motivated these two men on this day? Well, these men are just like us. We all have the same needs. We want acceptance. We want to be loved, we want to be valued, and we want to feel a sense of worth and purpose. In a way, I believe both men sought all this—especially justification before God.

The Pharisee sought his sense of value and worth from comparing himself to others and obeying the rules. But his sense of value and worth came from the comparison to and recognition he received from others. That should be good enough for God.

The tax collector already realized he was a lost cause. He knew himself, and he certainly wasn't going to get approval from men. If he were to have any hope for value and worth, it would have to come from God. And so, he threw himself on God's mercy. What did Lavan discover about God that day? He found that God is merciful to the humble and contrite. Jesus said this is the man who went home justified. And not only justified but lifted, full of joy! A demonstration of the Apostle James's words, "Humble yourselves before the Lord, and he will exalt you" (James 4:10).

## God Humbles the Proud

*You rescue the humble, but you humiliate the proud.*

—Psalm 18:27 NLT

"I'm going to fly you up to Teterboro, and Mike will fly you back." I boastfully said to our CEO as I greeted him at the airport in the fall of 1999. Although only the copilot, I had been checked out first on our new aircraft and was to fly this leg accompanied by Mike, my partner and captain in the right seat with a training captain observing. I boarded the aircraft only to discover the training captain in the left seat. He indicated we were running late, so he was going to take this leg. I sat in back with our passengers and the burst balloon of my deflated ego!

God is revulsed by pride. So much so that He makes it a point to humiliate the proud, the self-satisfied, the self-righteous. Like the flashing lights, clanging bells, and dropped barricade arms at a railroad crossing warn us of an approaching train, so myriad Bible passages warn us of the danger of pride. Attend to a few.

"You rescue the humble, but your eyes watch the proud and humiliate them" (2 Samuel 22:28 NLT).

"Though the Lord is great, he cares for the humble, but he keeps his distance from the proud" (Psalm 138:6 NLT).

"But he gives more grace. Therefore it says, 'God opposes the proud, but gives grace to the humble'" (James 4:6).

"Beware of practicing your righteousness before other people in order to be seen by them, for then you will have no reward from your Father who is in heaven. Thus, when you give to the needy, sound no trumpet before you, as the hypocrites do in the synagogues and in the streets, that they may be praised by others. Truly, I say to you, they have received their reward" (Matthew 6:1–2).

Why such warnings? Pride is the root of all sin. It seeks to elevate self above others, even God. It not only drives His distance but invites His ongoing opposition. It is the exact antithesis of what pleases God. The arrogance of a motorist who contests a two-hundred-ton locomotive at a barricaded railroad crossing with a one-ton car results in tragic consequences. Our pride invites even worse.

## Jesus Sets the Bar for Humility

*Have this mind among yourselves, which is yours in Christ
Jesus, who, though he was in the form of God, did not count
equality with God a thing to be grasped, but emptied himself, by taking the form of a servant, being born in the likeness of men. And being found in human form, he humbled
himself by becoming obedient to the point of death, even
death on a cross.*

—Philippians 2:5–8

If Jesus pleased God by His humility and obedience, should we
not take this attitude to heart as well? We can't imagine the glory
Jesus enjoyed, what it cost Him to humble himself, enduring nine
months of gestation, born in human flesh, rejecting all attempts
by the enemy and man to make Him a human king, and then to
accept a criminal's death dying horribly on the cross, assuming our
sin, our shame, to present us righteous before God and all Heaven.

Jesus said much to His disciples as they shared His last meal,
the Passover, together. However, He communicated His greatest
point not in words but action. The disciples had been arguing
over which of them was the greatest.ʷ Jesus removed His outer
garment, girded Himself with a towel, and, one by one, washed
His disciples' feet, an act normally performed by a house servant
welcoming invited guests. Jesus reinforced this, saying, "If I then,
your Lord and Teacher, have washed your feet, you also ought to
wash one another's feet" (John 13:14).

Can you identify? Have we ever found ourselves judging, if
even only internally, who was contributing most to a relationship,

---

ʷ This event is recorded in Luke's Gospel 22:24–27 as coinciding with the Last
Supper.

project, or mission, seeking to elevate ourselves, to justify our worth—completely oblivious to the fact that we are justified by Jesus alone, and anything accomplished in us is a result of God's working? I know I have.

Jack Deere, an American pastor and theologian, addressed our church in North Carolina while visiting in the early 1990s. "We have two choices. Either we can humble ourselves, or God will humble us. I prefer the former but will take it any way I can get it!"

A scene in Revelation, the last book of the Bible, depicts twenty-four elders, clothed in white—representing justification—sitting on twenty-four thrones representing authority, wearing gold crowns representing reward. And yet they cast their crowns before the throne of God, worshiping, recognizing He deserves all glory, not only for their justification but for their rewards as well.[x] What a warning to us to take a crowbar and sledgehammer to our pride and humbly receive our justification and commendation from Jesus.

*    *    *

Nothing crushes pride like living in a desert, wearing an itchy shirt with a hard leather belt, and living off insects and honey. So, this was the man whom God chose to announce the coming of His Son and prepare the way for His Kingdom. John, the son of Zechariah, dealt with doubt, held to hope, and caught the commendation of Christ overcoming life's greatest challenge, facing death. Let's learn from him as we see what he recognized about Jesus.

---

[x] This scene is recorded in Revelation 4.

*So Jesus said to the twelve, "Do you want to go away as well?" Simon Peter answered him, "Lord, to whom shall we go? You have the words of eternal life, and we have believed, and have come to know, that you are the Holy One of God."*

—John 6:67–69

I bless you, beloved proclaimer of Christ,
To hold steadfastly to what you have experienced
of Jesus,
Revealed to your spirit by the Father,
To stand for what is right,
In the face of opposition,
And when the discouragement of doubt assails you,
To take your questions to Jesus,
That He might remind of what you have experienced,
And what you have seen,
To hear His commendation,
And to receive the joy of His approval,
affirmation, and pleasure,
as you stand strong.

# Chapter 12

# None Is Greater

*Whoever finds his life will lose it, and whoever loses
his life for my sake will find it. —Jesus*

—Matthew 10:39

John wondered why he was still alive as he paced his prison
cell. That old goat Herod clearly wanted him dead. The
image of Herod's face, contorted in rage, when his soldiers had
dragged him away, stood seared in his mind even as the image of
an out-of-control fire portends the destruction ahead. John had
dared to denounce Herod for marrying his brother Philip's wife
in violation of Jewish law. A law that as king he was obligated to
uphold.

John contemplated this as he took two short steps to reach
the shaft of sunlight peering through a small, barred window. It
offered some meager warmth and illumination in the otherwise
stone cold and dark room. He rubbed his hands rapidly against
the chill. *That coward must be afraid of the Jews,* John reasoned.

The Jewish people held John in high esteem, and any further
move on Herod's part might spark riots that would bring the

wrath of Rome down on his head. Still, his shoulders drooped at the realization that each new day could be his last. John moved to the corner of the cell, his chill somewhat abated, and sat on the straw-covered stone slab, the only furnishing in the sparse quarters. That he still lived was not all that bewildered him. This young rabbi, Jesus, increasingly perplexed him—a confusion prompting him to send his disciples with questions.

He had seen it so clearly, if only for a moment. He had known from an early age he was set apart for something special. His father, Zechariah, never tired of telling him about the angel's appearance while serving in the temple. The angel had promised John would be like Elijah preparing the Jewish people for the coming of the Lord. A promise the angel had validated by striking his father mute when he had asked for proof. His father always told the story with a deep sense of wonder that captivated John, and yet with a twinkle in his eye at his own foolishness, which kept John from taking himself too seriously.

John had grown up around Jesus. As cousins, they saw each other occasionally when their parents would visit or travel to Jerusalem for a feast. They had enjoyed great fun playing together but had grown apart in later years. Jesus had apprenticed under his father Joseph as a carpenter while He studied the Torah with local rabbis. John had responded to his powerful sense of calling by going to the solitude of the desert, living a hermit's life, preaching to those who came, and baptizing those who responded in repentance.

John carried a deep burden. He expected the Messiah to soon appear among his people. And he knew his people, especially the religious leaders, were not ready. He must make them ready. Deep repentance was required in Israel before the One greater than him would appear.

The moment of clarity came suddenly and unexpectedly, like the shaft of sunlight that occasionally pierced through the clouds and streamed into his cell. It had been such an overcast day when the sun suddenly appeared. He had been preaching and baptizing by the Jordan. The power of God was especially strong. Many queued to enter the water, all broken with the conviction of repentance.

John had seen Jesus walking toward him and saw as he had never seen Him before. This was no mere carpenter, not even a promising young rabbi. This was...words failed him. And then they came. They came with such illumination, with such force, that John cried out, no more able to stop the words than a few bags of sand could stop a flash flood from a sudden spring storm. "Behold, the lamb of God, who takes away the sin of the world!" (John 1:29b).

Then, unthinkably, the One who had no need to repent, Jesus, had asked to be baptized by him. After protestations of unworthiness, John eventually consented. It had been a glorious day, the culmination of John's life and ministry. The One for whom John had prepared the way finally appeared.

Yet as vivid the picture, it was a distant memory as John sat in prison. He rose and walked slowly toward the shaft of sunlight as if seeking divine illumination. But it was not to be found as the shaft of light vanished, the sun's rays obscured by a passing cloud. And just as profoundly, the illumination John had received concerning Jesus was now gone. *Is He really the One? Did I miss it? Should I look for another?* Those were the questions John needed answered and the questions he had sent his disciples to ask.

As John turned back toward the slab, he heard a voice. "Master, master!" John turned to see Alpheus, one of his disciples, standing on the other side of the bars, accompanied by a large, scowling guard.

"Did you find Him?" asked John, his eyes wide and voice rising.

"Yes, yes, we gave Him your message."

"And His reply?"

"He said this: 'Go and tell John what you have seen and heard: the blind receive their sight, the lame walk, lepers are cleansed, and the deaf hear, the dead are raised up, the poor have good news preached to them'" (Luke 7:22).

John recognized the words, a reference from the prophet Isaiah concerning the Messiah.[y] A weight lifted. The lightness drew John back to that glorious day at the Jordan. "So, He is the One," said John. Then to himself, *My work was not in vain. Jesus truly is the Messiah, the Son of God.* But that is not what John had called Him at His baptism. The words that came specifically described Jesus as the "Lamb of God," who "takes away the sin of the world." These were hardly words one would use to describe the Messiah, the Son of God, a king. John briefly pondered the meaning and turned to Alpheus. "Is that it? Was there anything else?"

Alpheus hesitated, replying softly, "He said to tell you, 'Blessed is the one who is not offended by me'" (Luke 7:23).

John made his way to the front of the cell and carefully reached through the bars, firmly grasping Alpheus's shoulders as he looked deeply into his eyes. "Thank you, dear friend, thank you." John slowly released his grasp and turned back toward his bed. He knew what Jesus meant. John had been offended, if only temporarily. Things had not turned out as anticipated. Jesus did

---

[y] "Then the eyes of the blind shall be opened, and the ears of the deaf unstopped; then shall the lame man leap like a deer, and the tongue of the mute sing for joy. For waters break forth in the wilderness, and streams in the desert" (Isaiah 35:5–6).

not fit his picture of the Messiah King, the deliverer of Israel. Yet now, beyond a doubt, John knew. Jesus was the Messiah, the Son of God. And the Lamb of God who takes away the sins of the world. Whatever that would mean.

John would not hear the rest of what Jesus had said. Alpheus and the others had left Jesus and could not report what came next. But after they left, Jesus turned and addressed the crowd (as stated in Matthew 11:7b–11):

> What did you go out into the wilderness to see? A reed shaken by the wind? What then did you go out to see? A man dressed in soft clothing? Behold, those who wear soft clothing are in kings' houses. What then did you go out to see? A prophet? Yes, I tell you, and more than a prophet. This is he of whom it is written, "Behold, I send my messenger before your face, who will prepare your way before you." Truly, I say to you, among those born of women there has arisen no one greater than John the Baptist. Yet the one who is least in the kingdom of heaven is greater than he.

John would soon not hear at all anymore, after the sound of a key turning in the lock of his cell. He slowly rose and blinked. There stood two guards. One with his sword drawn, the other holding an empty serving platter. Nevertheless, John was at peace. His work was finished. He had been faithful to the Lord.

## Jesus Commends the Steadfast

*Praise the Lord! Oh give thanks to the Lord, for he is good, for his steadfast love endures forever!*

—Psalm 106:1

Jesus commends the steadfast. Why? Because steadfastness is a compelling quality of God. The word "steadfast" is used 132 times in the book of Psalms, over 120 times referring to God, His love, and His faithfulness. In Psalm 136, God's steadfast love is used as a refrain for each of the twenty-six verses. The emphasis is on God's faithfulness, not ours.

Any quality of God that we display is evidence we have received from Him, responded to His initiative. Consider Jesus's words as He commends John: "What did you go out into the wilderness to see? A reed shaken by the wind?" (Matthew 11:7b). It pleases Jesus immensely to see His qualities, those of the Father, manifested in our lives. This is evidence of an openness to receive from God. As in Flavius's demonstration of faith, Zacchaeus's vow of integrity, and Peter's confession of Jesus's divinity, Jesus receives much pleasure from those who get it. John's steadfast commitment to Jesus, His Kingdom and its values of repentance, adherence to God's moral imperatives, and refusal to compromise, elicited Jesus's approval and commendation. And John experienced joy in Jesus's pleasure.

## Jesus Commends Those Who Bring Their Doubts to Him

*Jesus said to her, "Did I not tell you that if you believed, you would see the glory of God?"*

—John 11:40

Do you have the same questions as I? Sometimes what we see of Jesus is not what we had expected. We had great hopes, believed He would act in a certain way, and like the football coach who calls for the same run up the middle from the one-yard line when the previous three tries failed, Jesus disappoints, appears ineffective in the face of our circumstances.

Both of our first two attempts at adoption, falling through at the last minute, left questions. And doubts. Was God leading us on, just to disappoint? Were we even capable of being parents? These were concerns we took back to God, along with our pain. John had questions. His expectation of the Messiah, one who would assume the throne of David and deliver Israel from Roman oppression, did not match what he saw of Jesus. What would he do?

As we have noted previously, faith must be tested. These tests are not unusual, more typical than not. This is hope forging perseverance. But here, the tests are different. John's faith test is not about Jesus providing a certain answer as in our move to Atlanta. The test is about Jesus Himself. Is Jesus actually who He claims to be, even when common sense says otherwise? Does He even care about our desire to have a child when our situation seems to scream otherwise? Oswald Chambers, a twentieth-century Scottish evangelist, describes this experience:

> Every time you venture out in your life of faith, you will find something in your circumstances that, from a commonsense standpoint, will flatly contradict your faith. But common sense is not faith, and faith is not common sense. In fact, they are as different as the natural life and the spiritual. Can you trust Jesus Christ where your common sense cannot trust Him?… Every time my theology becomes clear to my own mind, I encounter something that contradicts it… Faith must be tested because it can only become your intimate possession through conflict. What is challenging your faith right now? The test will either prove your faith right, or it will kill it. Jesus said, "Blessed is he who

is not offended because of Me" (Matthew 11:6). The ultimate thing is confidence in Jesus.[34]

How would John deal with his doubts, respond to this crisis of faith? By bringing his questions to Jesus. He didn't trust his preconception of how Jesus would act. He trusted Jesus to correct his assumptions. John looked his offense in the eye, stared down its attempt to isolate him from Jesus, and believed Jesus would bring light to the darkness of his doubt. John had confidence and took comfort in Jesus's answer. Jesus did not give him a full explanation. He does not do so for us. What did John recognize about Jesus this day? Jesus gave him enough to confirm His Messiahship. John may not have understood the significance of Jesus's eventual suffering, execution, and resurrection at the time. But as he was reminded of his declaration at Jesus's baptism, "Behold, the lamb of God, who takes away the sin of the world!" (John 1:29b), a dim light brightened. He had peace, even in the face of his impending death.

## Jesus Commends Those Clothed in His Righteousness

*Truly, I say to you, among those born of women there has arisen no one greater than John the Baptist. Yet the one who is least in the kingdom of heaven is greater than he.*
*—Jesus*

—Matthew 11:11

This is an amazing statement. Perfect righteousness sets a high bar. John came closer than anyone up to his time, of clearing it. He was filled with the Holy Spirit in the womb. His birth fulfilled prophecy. He held fast to the moral requirements of God. He devoted himself to Jesus's appearance, the Kingdom of God, and a passion to prepare people to possess it. Yet he still missed the bar. So, who are those in the Kingdom of Heaven, and how are they greater than John?

Would it surprise you to know that you, me, anyone who has trusted in Christ for forgiveness of sins, confessed Him as Lord, and has received the Holy Spirit, are those of the Kingdom of Heaven?[z] What makes us greater than John? Jesus cleared the bar of righteousness. He is the only one to have done it, the only one who ever will. He did not just clear it by inches but by gazillions of feet! This is the righteousness that is ours. It is not of our own making but received by faith for those who are in Christ.[aa]

*     *     *

Do you doubt Jesus's ability to forgive your sin, feel you don't have anything worthy of a commendation from Jesus? We'll now look at a man who is at the opposite extreme from John. Consider Dismas, a criminal sentenced to death, who encountered Jesus, experienced deep repentance, and developed a sudden intense distaste for the profane, yet received a commendation

---

[z] "And Peter said to them, 'Repent and be baptized every one of you in the name of Jesus Christ for the forgiveness of your sins, and you will receive the gift of the Holy Spirit. For the promise is for you and for your children and for all who are far off, everyone whom the Lord our God calls to himself'" (Acts 2:38–39).

[aa] "But God, being rich in mercy, because of the great love with which he loved us, even when we were dead in our trespasses, made us alive together with Christ—by grace you have been saved—and raised us up with him and seated us with him in the heavenly places in Christ Jesus, so that in the coming ages he might show the immeasurable riches of his grace in kindness toward us in Christ Jesus. For by grace you have been saved through faith. And this is not your own doing; it is the gift of God, not a result of works, so that no one may boast" (Ephesians 2:4–9).

from Jesus. His story, and what he recognized about Jesus, unfolds next.

*Truly, truly, I say to you, whoever hears my word and believes him who sent me has eternal life. He does not come into judgment, but has passed from death to life. —Jesus*

—John 5:24

I bless you, dear, beloved, hopeless one,
Who has nothing to offer,
But your desperation, brokenness, and faith,
To experience the hope of Jesus's promise,
"Today you will be with me in paradise."
I bless you to comprehend the significance
of the cross,
Though you have nothing to commend,
only a life of regret,
And no way to make up for the past.
Jesus's atoning sacrifice,
Has paid all you owe,
His perfect righteousness,
Is now yours.

# Chapter 13

# The Last Request

*But the Lord takes pleasure in those who fear him,*
*in those who hope in his steadfast love.*

—Psalm 147:11

*D*ismas's knees buckled under the load. The rough wooden beam lashed across his shoulders was heavy enough.[ab] The heavier burden of deep regret over a wasted life and his imminent, painful death caused the stagger.

Dismas and his associate Gestas had been seized three weeks prior by a local centurion. The consequences of a larcenous and murderous career finally caught up with them as they had chosen the wrong man as their latest victim. He had been a close friend of the centurion who wasted no time hunting them down. Their conviction and sentence were swift, death by

---

[ab] The story of the crucifixion of Jesus highlighting the repentance of one of the thieves is found in Luke's Gospel, Chapter 23:32–48, and unless otherwise noted, the dialogue is taken from this account. Though the names Dismas and Gestas are not mentioned in the biblical account, some historical records attribute these names to the two thieves crucified with Jesus.

crucifixion. After several delays, the day arrived. Dismas's initial bravado and curses hurled at his Roman guards had gradually diminished as the day approached and the reality of his demise grew large.

Dismas recovered his footing in time to feel the lash of the guard's whip urging him on. He couldn't even cry out as he looked at Gestas, carrying his beam and still cursing loudly at the soldiers and onlookers who had gathered to witness. He marveled at his partner's callous defiance. Dismas winced in revulsion, as if jabbed with a sharp knife, at each new insult cast indiscriminately at those nearby.

The third figure in their grim procession was barely recognizable, His face swollen and bleeding from blows and a wreath of thorns pushed into his head. He had been severely flogged as well, and by this point, weak from loss of blood, could no longer carry his cross. The soldiers conscripted an onlooker to carry it the remaining distance.

Dismas gazed wide-eyed at this man whose bearing and demeanor stood in stark contrast to Gestas. He knew His name, Jesus the Nazarene, a young rabbi under the same condemnation by Pilate at the demand of a crowd who had just lauded Him the previous day. Jesus's silence and calmness amid such torment fascinated Dismas. He radiated a peace even in anguish that Dismas wished he possessed. It was as if Jesus were embracing His fate, a thought incomprehensible.

The procession now approached the summit where a sharp rise in grade mocked the condemned as they struggled to reach the site of their execution. Dismas reluctantly labored against the slope as a mother halfheartedly pushes to deliver a stillborn baby. *Is that what I'm facing?* wondered Dismas. *Entry into whatever comes next as one born dead?* Dismas wasn't even sure of what came next. He hadn't given it much thought until now. Even the Jewish leaders were divided on this. The Pharisees acknowledged an afterlife. The Sadducees did not. But Dismas knew that whatever was to come, he wasn't ready.

What happened next happened quickly. The Roman soldiers were coldly efficient as they simultaneously nailed each prisoner's arms and feet to the cross beams and posts and hoisted the rough assemblages upright, dropping them in their holes with a jarring thud that ignited every nerve in Dismas's body. He cried out while Gestas screamed even more vehement curses. Jesus winced at each hammer stroke and gasped when His cross was erected but remained silent even as He was stripped bare. Jesus's silence suddenly broke. He uttered words incomprehensible to Dismas. "Father, forgive them, for they know not what they do."[ac]

*How could Jesus do this?* Dismas could not conceive what Jesus's crime had been. He heard Pilate had declared Jesus innocent, washing his hands of Jesus's blood. Whatever it was, Dismas knew Jesus did not deserve this. So why would an innocent man forgive his murderers? How would they respond to this forgiveness?

Dismas watched in horror as onlookers hurled insults. "You who would destroy the temple and rebuild it in three days, save yourself! If you are the Son of God, come down from the cross." Then even some of those forgiven, the Jewish chief priests, scribes, and Pharisees scoffed at Him.

One of the Temple rulers jeered, "He saved others; let him save himself, if he is the Christ of God, his Chosen One!" One by

---

[ac] The story and dialogue of Jesus's crucifixion is taken from Luke 23 and Matthew 27:32–54.

one, the others joined the chorus. It worsened. The soldiers joined in the mocking, offering him sour wine and taunts.

"If you are the King of the Jews, save yourself!" one shouted, referencing an inscription Pilate had ordered displayed over Jesus. Finally, even Gestas joined in, enjoying the momentary levity as a brief reprieve from his own torment.

"Are you not the Christ? Save yourself and us!"

Dismas could take it no longer. He exploded at Gestas, rising up against the pain to give his voice full volume. "Do you not fear God since you are under the same sentence of condemnation? And we indeed justly, for we are receiving the due reward of our deeds; but this man has done nothing wrong."

*Could this actually be the Christ?* Dismas turned toward Jesus with a look of both desperation and hope. Jesus gazed deeply into his eyes. Dismas sagged, struggling now to speak. "Jesus, remember me when you come into your kingdom."

Jesus responded, His words full of authority and compassion that belied His physical condition. "Truly, I say to you, today you will be with me in Paradise."

Dismas sobbed deeply. Was it possible that even his sins could be forgiven, that with no chance, no ability to redeem himself, that this dying man could speak into his heart with so much authority? Vision darkened for Dismas as he struggled to breathe. But as he tried for a final glimpse of Jesus, he realized it wasn't his eyes failing. The harsh noonday sun, beating down as relentlessly as the onlookers' taunting, vanished, hiding as if it could not bear to witness such foul deeds. Dismas looked at the mockers in amazement, their silence now as deep as the enveloping gloom.

Time disappeared as Dismas weakened, his life ebbing. Darkness and silence, only interrupted by his labored attempts at breathing, continued for three hours. Suddenly a loud cry pierced the silence, sending an intense chill over the now roused Dismas. "My God, my God, why have you forsaken me?"

Dismas would have jumped off the cross had he not been nailed down. These words of Jesus were familiar. He had heard them before. Words of King David from a collection of poetry his mother had read to him as an infant.[ad] He began to mouth them softly:

> My God, my God, why have you forsaken me?
> Why are you so far from saving me,
> from the words of my groaning?
>
> Yet you are holy, enthroned on the praises of Israel.
> In you our fathers trusted; they trusted, and you delivered them.
> To you they cried and were rescued; in you they trusted and were not put to shame.

---

[ad] Psalm 22 is one of myriad Old Testament prophecies fulfilled in Jesus's crucifixion, written before this method of execution had even been invented. In Science Speaks, Peter Stoner and Robert Newman discuss the statistical improbability of one man, whether accidentally or deliberately, fulfilling just eight of the prophecies Jesus fulfilled. The chance of this happening, they say, is one in ten to the seventeenth power. Stoner presents a scenario that illustrates the magnitude of such odds: Suppose that we take ten to the seventeenth silver dollars and lay them on the face of Texas. They will cover all of the state two feet deep. Now mark one of these silver dollars and stir the whole mass thoroughly, all over the state. Blindfold a man and tell him that he can travel as far as he wishes, but he must pick up one silver dollar and say that this is the right one. What chance would he have of getting the right one? Just the same chance that the prophets would have had of writing these eight prophecies and having them all come true in any one man, from their day to the present time, providing they wrote using their own wisdom. The mathematical improbability of three hundred, or forty-seven, or even just eight fulfilled prophesies of Jesus stands as evidence to his Messiahship. Science Speaks, Peter Stoner and Robert Newman, Online Edition, Revision Nov. 2005, Copyright © 2002, Donald Wayne Stoner, p. 50.

But I am a worm and not a man, scorned by mankind
and despised by the people.

All who see me mock me; they make mouths at me;
they wag their heads;

"He trusts in the Lord; let him deliver him; let him
rescue him, for he delights in him!"

I am poured out like water, and all my bones are out of joint;
my heart is like wax; it is melted within my breast;

my strength is dried up like a potsherd, and my tongue
sticks to my jaws;

you lay me in the dust of death.

For dogs encompass me; a company of evildoers encir-
cles me;

they have pierced my hands and feet

I can count all my bones—they stare and gloat over me;

they divide my garments among them,

and for my clothing they cast lots.

—Psalm 22:1, 3–8, 14–18

Dismas's gaze lowered, catching the soldiers marking small,
freshly cut branches, preparing to cast lots for Jesus's stripped robe.
Trembling, Dismas looked toward Him. Jesus's parched mouth
opened wide as Dismas caught His unmistakable last shout.

"Father, into your hands I commit my spirit!" Jesus slumped.
Dismas shook uncontrollably, yet the shaking came not from
within. The very ground rocked and his cross swayed. Sharp explo-
sions filled the air as stones split. Then another voice escaped the
cacophony of the awestruck crowd.

"Truly this man was the Son of God!" (Mark 15:39b).

Dismas followed the sound. There, at the foot of Jesus's cross, the centurion who had led the execution detail dropped to his knees and beat his chest. Many in the crowd followed.

*The Son of God. The Son of God.* As Dismas repeated this phrase, an overwhelming peace took hold, and he felt himself impossibly lifted from the cross. He did not feel the soldier's blows breaking his legs, ensuring his death before the sunset ushered in the Sabbath. He was somewhere else, no pain, no tears, only an indescribable, glorious light and presence of love. Dismas had no words. He only knew that, however undeserved, this is where he belonged.

Dismas would not be an earthly witness to the events of the next three days. He would not see Joseph of Arimathea request Jesus's body and place it in a tomb. Nor would he see the stone sealing the tomb rolled away or witness the resurrection of Jesus as did the disciples and over five hundred others. Time and his past no longer bound Dismas, as he basked in the glory of the living Christ and worshipped the One who had purchased his pardon.

*Truly, I say to you, today you will be with me in paradise.*
—*Jesus*

—Luke 23:43

What did Dismas discover about Jesus that day? This story stirs something deep within me. Dismas displayed many of the virtues we have seen Jesus commend. As others we have viewed, he recognized Jesus as the Messiah; he experienced deep regret at his spiritual poverty and repented, resisting the urge of pain-inspired verbal retaliation. He approached Jesus in desperation, humility, and faith, trusting Him for the hope of salvation. But there is something more here that speaks to me. Dismas had no chance to offer Jesus a changed life, to make things right as did Zacchaeus. Yet on this day, he was the first to recognize Jesus's righteousness, His divinity, and His Kingship over a greater realm.

Jesus's identity was clearly displayed throughout this ordeal, remarkably even by those who didn't acknowledge it, as if compelled to testify to the truth. The sign, "King of the Jews," placed over His head by Pilate and those who called Him "Son of God" while mocking speak to the irresistible assent to Jesus as Lord all will be compelled to make.[ae] His authority and divinity were displayed in the forgiveness offered by Jesus to those who performed this vile act, and recognized by the centurion who praised God, declaring, "Truly this man was the Son of God!" (Mark 15:39b).

The earthquake, darkening of the sky, the rending of the curtain barring entrance to the Holy of Holies in the Temple, the dead who came alive, and for those who had eyes to see, the fulfillment of prophecy, all confirmed Jesus as the Messiah of God.[af] But only Dismas received Jesus's promise of joining Him in paradise, receiving the commendation of eternal life.

## Jesus Commends Those Who Trust in Him Alone

Jesus commends those who, having nothing to offer, recognizing their spiritual poverty, trust Him alone for salvation. There is no

---

[ae] See Philippians 2:9–11, "Therefore God has highly exalted him and bestowed on him the name that is above every name, so that at the name of Jesus every knee should bow, in heaven and on earth and under the earth, and every tongue confess that Jesus Christ is Lord, to the glory of God the Father."

[af] Each of the Gospels record crucifixion of Jesus and His resurrection. Matthew's Gospel includes these miraculous signs attesting to Jesus's divinity and Messiahship as well (Matthew 27:45–54).

attempt to bargain here. No attempt to rationalize criminality. An encounter with the manifest Presence of Jesus leads to a recognition of who He is. This recognition leads to a realization of our spiritual poverty and promotes repentance. This repentance leads to an intense grief over, and distaste for, sin and the profane. And this repentance leads to a deep trust, despite a life of regret, that touches Jesus's heart and leads to an assurance of salvation. It is this assurance of our salvation and God's love for us that displaces all fear.[ag]

Before we move on, we must recognize that this salvation leads to what comes next, our motivation for acting, which is love. Without the experience of salvation, the forgiveness of sin, we are incapable of a love that receives a commendation from Jesus. And we will see that the deeper the forgiveness, the deeper the resulting love.

We will also notice a shift. In our preceding stories, each character sought something from Jesus and, even in the seeking, pleased Him and received a commendation. But as we move forward, those on display do not seek anything from Jesus. Rather, each seeks to present Him a gift out of deep gratitude. They see more than His divinity. They have been touched by His overwhelming love. And they seek to offer Him something in return.

Have you experienced this type of love? If not, don't be deterred. As you explore these stories, let His deep forgiveness, affirmation, and love wash over you. Hear His personal commendation to you. Do you desire to offer Jesus a deep gift of love in response? Let these stories guide. As we continue, a warning is appropriate. These expressions of love involve sacrifice, and often

---

[ag] "There is no fear in love, but perfect love casts out fear. For fear has to do with punishment, and whoever fears has not been perfected in love" (I John 4:18).

come with personal risk. However, as we transition from hope to love, the risk is worth it. Our hope in God does not fail. The Apostle Paul encourages us. "And this hope will not lead to disappointment. For we know how dearly God loves us, because he has given us the Holy Spirit to fill our hearts with his love" (Romans 5:5 New Living Translation). I hope you will stay with me as we proceed, for the reward of the joy of His pleasure is great.

*For this reason I bow my knees before the Father, from whom every family in heaven and on earth is named, that according to the riches of his glory he may grant you to be strengthened with power through his Spirit in your inner being, so that Christ may dwell in your hearts through faith—that you, being rooted and grounded in love, may have strength to comprehend with all the saints what is the breadth and length and height and depth, and to know the love of Christ that surpasses knowledge, that you may be filled with all the fullness of God.*

—Ephesians 3:14-19

I bless you, dear, beloved of God,
To know the love of God,
Which is beyond knowledge,
To be filled with the Holy Spirit,
To perceive the love of Christ by faith,
That it might dwell in you, ground you, and take root,
And overflow in fullness to others.

# Section 4

◆

## Love

## Chapter 14

# *Love: The Commended Motivation*

*So now faith, hope, and love abide, these three;*
*but the greatest of these is love.*

—1 Corinthians 13:13

## Love Is the Motivation Jesus Commends

*F*aith causes us to act. Hope keeps us moving forward. Love is the only commendable motivation for action, the only motivation having eternal significance, and the only motivation pleasing to God. So why is this motivation of love so critical? The Apostle John gets right to the meat when he says, "Anyone who does not love does not know God, because God is love" (1 John 4:8).

I spent half my teenage years in the late sixties, the generation of the 5th Dimension's "The Age of Aquarius," the Beatles' "All You Need Is Love," and Woodstock. It was an anything-goes era if you had love, whatever that meant. This is not what John is saying. God is not a warm, fuzzy feeling, an ethereal cosmic force of love floating around the universe in a Jimi Hendrix–type purple haze. John is not describing God's essence, which is Spirit. He is describing His essential nature.

## Love Is God's Essential Nature

The Father's essential nature, the core of His identity, is love. It is more than just His highest quality. The Bible contains many descriptions of God. He is characterized as merciful, forgiving, kind, patient, just, omniscient, omnipresent, and more. However, He is not described as loving. Listen to the Apostle John, Jesus's most intimate friend, in his portrayal. "Beloved, let us love one another, for love is from God, and whoever loves has been born of God and knows God. Anyone who does not love does not know God, because God is love" (1 John 4:7–8).

John defines God as love itself and as the source of all love. Therefore, love is His motivation for His every action. Jesus's motivation is to bring glory to the Father by revealing the Father's nature; therefore, His motivation is love. What else would motivate Him to leave His throne in Heaven, endure a nine-month gestation, live in human flesh subject to all our common temptations, overcome sin, die a gruesome death, redeeming humanity and reconciling us to the Father, before He returned to His throne in Glory, having defeated and shamed His enemies by His resurrection?[ah] As love becomes our motivation for action, we reflect God's nature. This brings Him great joy and pleasure. It is the expression of our love to His Son, Jesus, which most pleases and blesses Him. Consider again John's words:

---

[ah] "And you, who were dead in your trespasses and the uncircumcision of your flesh, God made alive together with him, having forgiven us all our trespasses, by canceling the record of debt that stood against us with its legal demands. This he set aside, nailing it to the cross. He disarmed the rulers and authorities and put them to open shame, by triumphing over them in him (Colossians 2:13–15).

"Anyone who does not love does not know God, because God is love" (1 John 4:8). He highlights our ability to love as the litmus test for knowing God. And as we have observed previously, knowing God, and being known by Him is the basis for Jesus's commendation.

The Apostle Paul takes us deeper in his first letter to the Corinthian Church. "If I speak in the tongues of men and of angels, but have not love, I am a noisy gong or a clanging cymbal. And if I have prophetic powers, and understand all mysteries and all knowledge, and if I have all faith, so as to remove mountains, but have not love, I am nothing. If I give away all I have, and if I deliver up my body to be burned, but have not love, I gain nothing" (1 Corinthians 13:1–3).

These words might sound familiar. Ministers often recite them at wedding ceremonies as encouragement to the new husband and wife. But catch the significance of Paul's entreaty. He doesn't just say we gain nothing if we don't have love, but emphasizes we are nothing if our motivation is not love. We are empty; our identity is blank; we are cancelled. John and Paul tell us our true identity is defined in our relationship with and our knowledge of God, and the motivation of love is its manifestation.

## Love Is the Essential Nature of Jesus's Commands

The week leading to Jesus's crucifixion witnessed increased conflict. Jesus did not try to hide as He taught in the temple, directing much of His teaching against the Pharisees and their attempts at verbal entrapment. One young scribe, impressed with Jesus's answers, approached Him.[ai]

---

[ai] This story, and the dialogue, is chronicled by the disciple Mark and taken from Mark 12:28–34.

"Which commandment is the most important of all?"

Jesus answered, "The most important is, 'Hear, O Israel: The Lord our God, the Lord is one. And you shall love the Lord your God with all your heart and with all your soul and with all your mind and with all your strength.' The second is this: 'You shall love your neighbor as yourself.' There is no other commandment greater than these."

"You are right, Teacher. You have truly said that He is one, and there is no other besides Him. And to love Him with all the heart and with all the understanding and with all the strength, and to love one's neighbor as oneself, is much more than all whole burnt offerings and sacrifices."

"You are not far from the Kingdom of God," said Jesus.

As Jesus's answers impressed this scribe, so the scribe's response touched Jesus's heart. And Jesus commended him.

Jesus commanded much and expected obedience from His followers as a demonstration of their love for Him. Yet He distilled all the commandments to loving God and others as expressed in His last words to His disciples: "This is my commandment, that you love one another as I have loved you."[35] Why this emphasis? Certainly, all of God's law would be fulfilled if we loved perfectly as He. This simplification holds a deeper reason. Bill Johnson, Senior Pastor of Bethel Bible Church, explains, "We do well to pursue according to His commands. But romance is no longer romance when it is commanded."[36] As important as are all of Jesus's commands, His desire is for the intimacy of relationship motivated by love. This gives Him the greatest joy and pleasure. Before we move on, there are two more mind-boggling characteristics of God's love we need to consider.

# God's Love Transcends Human Comprehension

Are you having difficulty wrapping your arms around this type of love? Welcome to the club! Love of this quality is beyond human comprehension. So how do we grasp it? The Apostle Paul enlightens us in Ephesians 3:14–19.

> For this reason I bow my knees before the Father, from whom every family in heaven and on earth is named, that according to the riches of his glory he may grant you to be strengthened with power through his Spirit in your inner being, so that Christ may dwell in your hearts through faith—that you, being rooted and grounded in love, may have strength to comprehend with all the saints what is the breadth and length and height and depth, and to know the love of Christ that surpasses knowledge, that you may be filled with all the fullness of God.

Did you catch that? Paul describes Jesus's love in four dimensions and beyond knowledge. How then are we to understand it with a human three-dimensional mind? The Apostles John and Paul share their thoughts.

## God Loves Us First

*We love because he first loved us.*

—1 John 4:19

The key to grasping the love of God is to realize He loves us first. We don't earn it. We give up trying to prove something. It is not revealed through human understanding or human effort. It is revealed spiritually. Consider Paul's words again: "That according to the riches of his glory he may grant you to be strengthened with power through his Spirit in your inner being, so that Christ may dwell in your hearts through faith" (Ephesians 3:16–17a).

The Holy Spirit reveals God's love in our hearts as we abide in Jesus. John tells us how this works: "Whoever confesses that Jesus is the Son of God, God abides in him, and he in God. So we have come to know and to believe the love that God has for us. God is love, and whoever abides in love abides in God, and God abides in him. By this is love perfected with us" (1 John 4:15–17a).

God's love is greater than we can imagine. It is personally experienced, inwardly perceived, revealed to those who by faith confess the Lordship of Jesus at the invitation of the abiding Holy Spirit, and received as a gift, not earned. Brennan Manning highlights Walter Kasper's beautiful summary:

> German theologian Walter Kasper, after noting that personal experience is the sine qua non of biblical faith, concludes, "Experiencing God's love in Jesus Christ means experiencing that one has been unreservedly accepted, approved and *infinitely* loved [italics mine], that one can and should accept oneself and one's neighbor."[37] Trust, grounded in faith and hope, reaches an unprecedented level in the experience of infinite love. It is useless to protest that such a concept is too big for us. Of course it is too big for us. The kabōd Yahweh, the absolute glory of God, is revealed in Jesus as absolute love, and we can only be brushed by it. Nevertheless, we are made for that which is too big for us. We are made for God, and nothing less will ever satisfy us.[38]

The experience of the fullness of God's love would overwhelm us in this world and is meant for the next. Nevertheless, we are meant to live in it as it touches us in increasing measure in this world as revealed by the Holy Spirit, imparted to others, and returned to Him in deep gratitude.

## The Look of Love

The love of God is a weighty reality. It is first perceivable, taking on flesh, as we look at Jesus. But what does our love for Him look like? The following stories give form as we look at those whose expressions of love brought Jesus immense joy and pleasure and brought the joy of the assurance of His pleasure in return. A poor, elderly widow will lead the way as her silent actions loudly proclaim what she knows of God.

*So also you have sorrow now, but I will see you again, and your hearts will rejoice, and no one will take your joy from you. —Jesus*

—John 16:22

I bless you, beloved of God,
To be so filled with the joy of His love,
That you would overflow with thankfulness,
That even in great loss,
You would know the comfort and security,
Of God's love,
And know He takes great pleasure,
In your sacrificial gift of returned love,
No matter how small.

# Chapter 15

## All She Had

*Oh give thanks to the Lord, for he is good,*
*for his steadfast love endures forever!*

—Psalm 107:1

Miriam waited until the right moment to approach the offering box. She had hesitated, embarrassed by the little she had to bring. But now, as no one noticed, she made her move. She moved cautiously, slowed by age and the desire to avoid attention, yet with great anticipation, bearing her gift for her beloved.

She had been widowed many years earlier but was not alone. God had become her husband. Like a summer shower on a hot afternoon, He had washed away the dust of her loneliness and refreshed her with His Presence, leaving a lush green radiance in place of the dry foliage of her life.

And now, with great joy and thankfulness, she brought all that she had. She kissed the two small coins, dropped them quickly in the box, and turned to leave, her face radiant, hoping no one had noticed her private moment. No one had. No one had paid the slightest attention to this poor widow as she offered her gift. No one, that is, but Jesus, who sat quietly nearby, observing those who gave. This young rabbi often noticed that which others missed. He had a way of seeing into the heart, seeing beyond appearances.

He observed others, well dressed, timing their approach to the offering box to attract the greatest attention. They would linger over the box, depositing large sums of money, carefully dropping their coins one at a time to create the greatest effect. They made quite an impression on others, but not on Jesus. In fact, in just a few days' time, some of these wealthy donors would be demanding Jesus's crucifixion.

So, what did Jesus see in this woman that caused Him to take notice, to comment and commend? It was the faith born of her love and devotion to God. She had just given everything she had to live on, all that remained, with nothing left to offer. Yet she fully trusted her Beloved to meet her needs, which enabled her to put her very life in His hands with this act of returned love.

This touched something deep inside Jesus. He was familiar with the story of the widow of Zarephath, who had given the prophet Elijah her last meal, saw her supplies multiply, and later received her son, raised from the dead. He smiled.

How gracious of His Father to send encouragement. Jesus had recently predicted His death three times to His disciples. They heard the words but had not understood. And now, He prepared to share the Passover with them. It would be His last meal. He would share with them how He would give all he had, His body given for them, His blood to write a new covenant. Just as the widow of Zarephath offered her last meal to Elijah in obedience to God and saw her son raised from the dead as a result.

Just as this poor widow poured out all she had in an act of devotion to her beloved, Jesus would pour Himself out on the cross for the sins of the world. He would put all He had into His Father's hands, His very life, trusting that three days later, His Father would raise Him from the dead.

Jesus turned to His disciples, His voice filled with emotion, matching His fading smile. "You see that woman?" He asked. "She has given more than all the rest." Then wistfully, "All she had to live on." The words caught in His throat.[aj]

## Jesus Commends a Sacrificial Devotion That Trusts

What was the source of Miriam's joy? She had just given the last remaining resources on which, in Jesus's words, she had to live. Notice He did not say "on which she depended to live." Miriam's dependence was not on her assets, as meager as they were. What did Miriam recognize about God that day? She already knew Him and understood His deep, abiding, protective love. Her assurance was in God who had never let her down. More than that, He had met her every need for love, filling the empty pit of her loneliness. Her offering did not contribute to a cause but gifted the Giver who had been her delight. She gave in response to His love. This trust is greater than what we have heretofore explored. It is trust at its highest level. It was not a trust in God to do something for her. It was a trust that found its deepest joy in God Himself. Jesus commends great love that expresses itself in a great devotion and sacrifice that trusts. A trust that touched His heart.

---

[aj] The story of the poor widow and Jesus's words of commendation is recorded in Mark's Gospel (Mark 12:41–44). Some of the dialogue is paraphrased as it imagines how this touched Jesus deeply.

## Jesus Commends the Size of the Heart, Not the Size of the Gift

If Miriam was embarrassed at what little she had to offer, God was not. Of all who had given out of their abundance that day, Jesus commended only Miriam. In fact, commending her for having given more than all the others.

Even as I write, the memory of a day my heart was too small brings regret. My twenty-five-year-old son Daniel and I had just left Walmart when a homeless man approached, requesting money for a sleeping bag. Daniel had his own struggles and possessed limited resources. I rebuffed the man, but Daniel offered him ten dollars. My pride and pleasure in Daniel's response was only matched by the remorse of my refusal. Though cautious about giving money to strangers, I could have easily bought the man a sleep sack.

## Jesus Commends Those Who Seek to Please God, Not Man

Miriam purposed her gift to please God, not acquire approval from others. Jesus loved this. Consider His words recorded by Matthew: "Thus, when you give to the needy, sound no trumpet before you, as the hypocrites do in the synagogues and in the streets, that they may be praised by others. Truly, I say to you, they have received their reward. But when you give to the needy, do not let your left hand know what your right hand is doing, so that your giving may be in secret. And your Father who sees in secret will reward you" (Matthew 6:2–4).

Jesus does not elaborate on the Father's reward. The Bible does not record what Miriam received. It doesn't matter. Those who give freely, not to seek attention but out of a desire to bless the Father, trust He will supply what is needed. This trust brings Him extraordinary joy.

\* \* \*

Great forgiveness results in great love. We'll look through the eyes of a woman who offered Jesus extravagant worship at great risk and received a commendation for her great love. Her story is next. Let's see what Mary discovered about Jesus.

> *Therefore I tell you, her sins, which are many, are forgiven—for she loved much. But he who is forgiven little, loves little. —Jesus*
>
> —Luke 7:47

I bless you, beloved of God,
To approach Jesus with your shame and regrets,
To sense and receive the greatness of His love,
And forgiveness,
For you.
I bless you with the joy,
Of extravagant worship,
And oblivious to those around you,
To be drawn fully to Jesus,
To receive His commendation,
For your gift of ministry to Him,
To experience the joy of His pleasure,
And to have your lost innocence
Restored.

# Chapter 16

## A Lost Innocence Restored

*As far as the east is from the west, so far does he remove
our transgressions from us.*

—Psalm 103:12

"He's at Simon's House. Go see Him if you dare!" The unexpected words, as much of a taunt as information, startled Mary like a douse of cold water and at the same time chilled her. She turned to hear Salome, a professional colleague. "Well, you've been talking about Him. What are you waiting for?"

*It's true. I have been talking about Him, and now He's here?* Mary's pulse quickened.

Mary was increasingly disillusioned with the profession she and Salome shared. If you could call it a profession. The meeting of a need—for money, even good money—left her unsatisfied and empty. Certainly, the women of the community shunned her, and the men in the community, many her clients in private, publicly condemned her. She was used to that. But she could no longer justify what she knew was wrong.

But more than all that, the emptiness resulting from never having experienced true love, and the hopelessness of realizing she never would, left a constant ache she could not soothe. She was well aware of a brokenness she could no longer deny. And now she was trapped, as if caught in a giant whirlpool that sucked her further and further down, preventing escape from a life she detested.

Yet, like a glimpse of the sun's rays slicing through the murky depths of her despair, Mary saw hope in this young rabbi. Unlike other rabbis, He was known for associating with sinners, welcoming them, and even eating with them. Mary had vowed that if she ever had a chance, she would go to Him, to see for herself what Jesus might offer.

Yes, she had been talking about Him. But a problem emerged like an ugly weed looming in an otherwise beautiful flower garden. This Simon, at whose house Jesus could be found, was a Pharisee. To approach Jesus, in Simon's own house, would result in extreme public scorn, condemnation, and possibly death.

Mary's resolve strengthened. She would seek Him. She unthinkingly grabbed the jar containing her most costly perfume and hurried toward Simon's house. She had no plan, didn't know what she would say to Jesus if in fact she found Him, but a compulsion carried her. As she went, she began to feel a lightness, as if the afternoon sun, which seemed strangely brighter than usual, cut through the gloom of her desolation.

Suddenly, she was there, the scent of fresh-roasted lamb wafting from the doorway. The lively conversation and laughter from within gave way to a sudden silence as she entered, every eye now turned toward her. But Mary, unaware of the scrutiny, noticed a foot bowl at the entrance, its water clear and shimmering, unusual for so many guests. Her eyes fastened on Jesus as He reclined at the table in silence. As He looked at Mary, a sense of His love overwhelmed her. A love seemingly ignorant of her reputation, even though Mary knew that He knew. It was a love directed right at her that enveloped her like a warm blanket on a chilly night.

Mary wept. Then she went to Him, kneeling by the table, and suddenly noticed through misty eyes His unwashed, bare feet, standing in stark contrast to His holiness. The flow increased as she knelt over Him, the dark-spotted stains of her tears on His feet now becoming rivers washing the dust to the floor. She bent lower, drying Jesus's feet with her hair, began to kiss them, and then, recklessly, broke open her jar of expensive perfume, that which she had used to attract her clients, and poured it all out over Jesus's feet. She would no longer need it.

Mary became aware of the critical glare, previously focused her way, now turned toward Jesus. Did this prophet not know who this woman was? And if so, why did He allow her to touch Him? What would He do?

Jesus, sensing the thoughts of those present, turned toward His host. "Simon, I have something to say to you."

And he answered, "Say it, Teacher."

"A certain moneylender had two debtors. One owed five hundred denarii, and the other fifty. When they could not pay, he cancelled the debt of both. Now which of them will love him more?"

"The one, I suppose, for whom he cancelled the larger debt."

Jesus said to him, "You have judged rightly."

Jesus turned toward Mary and said to Simon, "Do you see this woman? I entered your house; you gave me no water for my feet, but she has wet my feet with her tears and wiped them with her hair. You gave me no kiss, but from the time I came in she has not ceased to kiss my feet. You did not anoint my head with oil, but she has anointed my feet with ointment. Therefore I tell you, her sins, which are many, are forgiven—for she loved much. But he who is forgiven little, loves little."

Jesus turned toward Mary. "Your sins are forgiven."

Then those at the table with Him began to say among themselves, "Who is this, who even forgives sins?"

But Mary knew. This was not just any rabbi, not just any prophet; this was the Messiah, the Son of God. Suddenly she was clean, as clean as the feet she had just washed, and as fragrant to God as the perfume she had just poured out on Jesus's feet. Then Jesus said, still looking at her, "Your faith has saved you; go in peace."[ak]

## Jesus Commends Great Worship Arising from Great Forgiveness and Love

What prompted Mary's extravagant expression of love and worship for Jesus, an expression that baffled and offended Simon and his guests? What did she experience that they did not? And what led Mary to choose her profession?

The opening scene in Dallas Jenkins's drama *The Chosen* depicts a different Mary as her father reads the words of Isaiah the prophet to her as a young girl.[39] "But now thus says the Lord, he who created you, O Jacob, he who formed you, O Israel: 'Fear not, for I have redeemed you; I have called you by name, you are mine'" (Isaiah 43:1).

Fast-forward to Mary's adult years. She is found in a tavern, called by a different name, desperately seeking to free herself from her life as a demon-possessed prostitute, asking for a drink to bring it to an end. She encounters Jesus before the proprietor

---

[ak] This story of great forgiveness and some of the dialogue is chronicled in the Holy Bible, Luke 7:36–50.

can serve. She rebuffs His intervention at first, until He speaks one more time. "Mary, I have called you by name; you are mine." Mary sobs as Jesus hugs her, freeing her from her demonic bondage and giving her a new life.

We are not told what led Mary down her chosen path. We don't know what stole the innocence of the child in her daddy's arms and awakened the capacity for sin. Neither do we know what led the Mary who encountered Jesus in Simon's house to her occupation. Was it abuse, abandonment, or just a self-will and rebellion of which we are all guilty? It is of no import. What did Mary discover about Jesus that day? The Bible uses four different Greek words for love. Understanding two of these will give us insight. The word "eros" describes the erotic form of love; it is what dominated Mary's life. However, it left her empty. Eros only finds meaning when in partnership with "agape." Agape is the Greek word for a sacrificial, unconditional love. It is that which is used to describe God's love, and it is what Mary was missing until that day. It was agape love, and its accompanying unconditional forgiveness, that Mary found worthy of extravagant worship. Jesus's great love restored Mary's lost innocence. Bill Johnson observes:

> Great sinners have lost their innocence in so many areas of their lives. But for most of them, there remains deep in their hearts an innocence as it pertains to the Holy Spirit Himself. For most caught in deep sin, this part of the heart is still virgin territory. I've seen it so many times. The most corrupt, the most immoral and deceptive, are changed in a moment when the Holy Spirit comes upon them. Under all the callousness caused by sin was a place of deep tenderness. It is a place that none of us can see without help from the Holy Spirit.

Amazingly, their hearts responded to God when He showed up. It's the ones Jesus referred to when He said, "Therefore I tell you, her sins, which are many, are forgiven—for she loved much. But he who is forgiven little, loves little" (Luke 7:47). And it's that response that declares they are worthy of the dove. Conversely, it is often those who have been overexposed to the things of God that actually build a resistance to Him.[40]

I have seen this as well, having had the privilege to serve on teams with several churches in our community to walk alongside those in prison and in addiction recovery. Some of the greatest joy and softness is displayed in these dear ones who have found deep forgiveness and freedom in Christ. Jesus offered Mary a great forgiveness and a restored innocence for which she expressed an extravagant love-fueled worship that Simon could not comprehend—an expression of love Jesus commended and rewarded.

## Jesus Commends Great Worship Unrestrained

Great worship is extravagant, considering neither price nor perception. It is unrestrained and is God-conscious, not self-conscious. Any awkwardness Mary felt quickly disappeared as she focused on Jesus. She was no longer aware of the hostile crowd, consumed by what they might think of her. All her attention focused like a laser on Jesus. She sought only to minister to Him, to bless Him.

It has been said that ministering to Jesus is our first, foremost, and highest calling as His followers. It is our greatest assignment. Worship is not about us. It is not a feel-good pursuit. It is not something we drum up. It is a natural outflow and response to the love and forgiveness Jesus offers and is only revealed by the Holy Spirit. The greater our understanding of this love and forgiveness, the greater the expression of our worship. Mary offered Jesus personal ministry at great personal risk and sacrifice. A gift that brought Jesus immense joy and which He commended.

*     *     *

Jesus commends those who prioritize His Presence over presentation. We will look next at a woman who believed time in Jesus's Presence was not a waste, that everything else would take care of itself, fall into its correct place when she put seeking Jesus first. But we will see through the eyes of her sister. As we look at these two sisters, we will see one seeking Jesus's approval through service and one not seeking His approval at all, just soaking in His Presence. And we will learn what they both discovered about Jesus.

*As the Father has loved me, so have I loved you. Abide in my love. —Jesus*

—John 15:9

Dear beloved of God,

Your desire to please Jesus is commendable,

I bless you to receive understanding,

Of what truly blesses Him,

I bless you with the joy,

Of sitting in His Presence,

The freedom of ceasing your striving,

I bless you with the pleasure,

Of bringing Him pleasure,

As you take in all He has to offer,

And find your joy in His commendation,

For choosing the better part.

# Chapter 17

## The Better Part

*I am the vine; you are the branches. Whoever abides in me
and I in him, he it is that bears much fruit, for apart from
me you can do nothing. —Jesus*

—John 15:5

Martha violently attacked the meat with her knife, cutting precise pieces as she prepared the meal. She had initially been excited to learn of Jesus's Presence in Bethany and His plans, last minute though they were, to come to her home. She had rushed to begin meal preparations befitting such an honored guest, wanting to please Him above all, and had joyfully accepted her sister Mary's help as they discussed His anticipated visit with great animation.[al]

---

[al] Jesus's visit to Mary and Martha is contained in Luke 10:38–42 and is not described in detail. I have imagined how this might have unfolded, but it is not part of the biblical narrative.

The strife ironically began with Jesus's arrival. Before Martha could react, Mary had rushed to the door to welcome Him, almost tripping over the wash basin on her way.

*That should have been my place as the oldest,* Martha brooded as she made her way to the entrance, forcing a half-hearted greeting through a tight-lipped smile. *I'll give her a piece of my mind when we get alone.* Martha stomped back to the courtyard area used for cooking, while Mary led Jesus to a shady corner.

Then it worsened. Rather than returning to help, Mary sat down at Jesus's feet while He conversed with their brother Lazarus, soaking up every word of Jesus like a dry potted plant soaks up a pitcher of water.

*That's exactly what she looks like.* Martha sulked. *A potted plant, sitting in the middle of the floor and just as out of place. Doesn't she know that she should help prepare the meal while Lazarus keeps Jesus company?* Martha continued to fret. *The meal should have already been on the table when Jesus arrived. What must Jesus be thinking? Why doesn't He tell her to get over here and help me?*

Martha now attacked the meat with increasing vengeance, launching pieces at the stew pot like one might launch blows at a mocker, as the boiling water mimicked her volatile mood. She cast a glance at the corner of the courtyard. Mary continued to sit, her face peacefully radiant as she hung on Jesus's every word.

Martha flung the last piece of meat at the pot and stormed over. She assailed Jesus, one hand gesturing toward Mary while the other thrust toward Jesus, a lone finger wagging up and down like a serpent ready to strike. "Lord, do you not care that my sister has left me to serve alone?" Martha's words sliced through the air as her knife had sliced through the meat. "Tell her then to help me!"

Mary and Lazarus stared open-mouthed at Martha as her words hung in the stunned silence of the room like dirty linens hang in the still morning air. *How will Jesus respond to this rebuke?* They looked first at Jesus, then at Martha, then back at Jesus.

Jesus reached for Martha's outstretched hand as His eyes pierced her soul. "Martha, Martha, you are anxious and troubled about many things, but one thing is necessary. Mary has chosen the good portion, which will not be taken away from her." Jesus's gentle but firm words cooled the heated atmosphere as an afternoon shower soothes on a hot day and softened the hardened ground of Martha's angry heart.

## Jesus Commends Those Who Abide in Him

Jesus commends those who prioritize attendance over activity. We often have distorted ideas about what brings Him pleasure. Serving Jesus can distract us from Jesus. This distraction leads us to believe Jesus does not care. Believing Jesus does not care prevents us from enjoying Him and leads to a resentment toward those who are. Pastor Jack Frost shares a personal lament:

> No amount of fasting or study or servitude can earn the love of the Father, especially when the motivation behind these actions is based on a desire for personal gain and reward. As the weight of pleasing the Father became heavier and heavier on my shoulders, I sought release from the burden, by looking down on others not as disciplined as I was, in order to make me look good. I spent a great deal of time and energy on achieving excellence in myself, and I came to expect that same level of commitment from my family, my

congregation, and everyone else around me. When I placed my exacting standards on other people and found them to be lacking, my own ego was inflated and my spirituality seemed that much more holy, more pious, and more perfect than theirs. I was blind to my own self-deception.[41]

Our life will be characterized either by frenzied activity, anxiety and resentment, or abiding and peace. Abiding in Jesus is the answer, and bears much fruit, especially the joy of the Father's pleasure.

## Jesus Commends Those Who Bear Much Fruit

What if we actually accomplish more for Christ's Kingdom when we prioritize abiding in Him over activity? It is the night of Jesus's betrayal, and He is sharing His most intimate thoughts with His disciples. Hear His heart, as recorded in John 15:4–9.

Abide in me, and I in you. As the branch cannot bear fruit by itself, unless it abides in the vine, neither can you, unless you abide in me. I am the vine; you are the branches. Whoever abides in me and I in him, he it is that bears much fruit, for apart from me you can do nothing. If anyone does not abide in me he is thrown away like a branch and withers; and the branches are gathered, thrown into the fire, and burned. If you abide in me, and my words abide in you, ask whatever you wish, and it will be done for you. By this my Father is glorified, that you bear much fruit and so prove to be my disciples. As the Father has loved me, so have I loved you. Abide in my love.

There is much more Jesus would say and do this evening. He would tell them He was going away, and He would later return; He would tell them about the Holy Spirit whom He would send, and He would pray for them. After Jesus's resurrection, He would tell them to return to Jerusalem and wait until they received power from Heaven, the promise of the Father, the Holy Spirit.[am]

Jesus had risen from the dead and ascended into Heaven before their eyes. And then told them to wait. If I had seen this, I would probably have booked a stadium, put up billboards, and bought radio spots announcing a big revival. Good thing I wasn't there! The disciples obeyed Jesus, spent ten days abiding and praying together, and the next day saw three thousand souls launch Christ's Church.

The tension between abiding and moving, waiting and acting, being and doing, exists throughout the biblical narrative. But worship and abiding always takes precedence over activity and is the precursor to an exponential move of God.

## An Encounter with Jesus Transforms

So, what happened to Martha? What did she discover about Jesus that day? Did this encounter with Jesus change her? You cannot have a genuine encounter with Jesus and not be changed. You will either be drawn to Him and experience deeper joy or—in the case of an enthusiastic, rich, young ruler, dismayed by Jesus's request to sell his possessions—be unwilling to pay the price to follow, and go away saddened.

Although Martha came away changed, she discovered that Jesus's love for her never changed. He loved her at her worst as

---

[am] Jesus's last words to his disciples are chronicled in John chapters 15–17. Acts 1:4–8 chronicles Jesus's last words before his ascension, concerning their mission and the promise of the impending arrival of the Holy Spirit.

much as He loved her at her best. Jesus's love for us at our worst is what is so transforming! Have you ever had a day that started well, with much excitement, and then went rapidly south with an increasingly bad attitude, resulting in words you wish you could take back? Our initial response to the regret and embarrassment we experience on such occasions is to hide from God, as did Adam and Eve in the Garden of Eden. Yet as God covered the nakedness of Adam and Eve with animal skins, as He covered the Prodigal Son slimed in pig slop with a royal robe, He wraps us in His love. A love expressed in Jesus's gracious response to Martha's tirade, and a love that He would shortly express in His death on the cross to cover the slimy slop of our sin. Let's look at how this expression of Jesus's love impacted Martha, causing her to run toward Him, not away.

Sometime later, during Jesus's final weeks on Earth, Martha's brother Lazarus died. It was Martha mentioned first in John's account: "Now Jesus loved Martha and her sister and Lazarus" (John 11:5).

It was Martha, not Mary, who would be the first to go to Jesus when He returned to Bethany. She went not as one seeking approval this time but as one in desperate pain, in desperate need. She went to Jesus and laid all this at His feet.

It was Martha who would proclaim with great faith that not only could Jesus have prevented Lazarus's death but that even now, God would answer His prayer for Lazarus's resurrection—and He did! And it was Martha who would proclaim Jesus as the Messiah, the Son of God, a proclamation recorded by the Apostle John.[an]

Are we more concerned with our presentation or our presence? Do we maintain a healthy balance between the importance

---

[an] The Apostle John devotes much room for the story of Lazarus' death and resurrection after four days and is chronicled in John 11:1-44.

of preparation and then enjoy whatever it is we've prepared for? Are we able to put everything on pause in our worlds so we can simply sit at the feet of Jesus?

I have good news for you. God loves you. You are worth everything to Him. So much so that He sent His Son, Jesus, to die on the cross in your place, to purchase your pardon, to set you free from sin! Let's get personal here. God's love is not abstract. John records Jesus's conversation with the seeking Pharisee, Nicodemus, earlier in his Gospel. "For God so loved the world, that he gave his only Son, that whoever believes in him should not perish but have eternal life" (John 3:16).

But now John describes Jesus's love as specific. It narrows from the world to three individuals. "Now Jesus loved Martha and her sister and Lazarus" (John 11:5).

Let's narrow this down further, to one person. Jesus directs His love toward you. It is just as true to write "God loves," and you can insert your name here, as saying He loves the world, or Martha and Mary. And, as Martha discovered, He loves you at your worst! Receive and abide in His love. This brings Him immense pleasure.

## Jesus's Greatest Commendation

Jesus gives a great commendation to one who loved and forgave those who persecuted Him. He reflected Jesus's love and character so much that Jesus stood in honor of his death. His name is Stephen, and his story is next. Let's see what he discovered about Jesus.

*And do not fear those who kill the body but cannot kill the soul. Rather fear him who can destroy both soul and body in hell. —Jesus*

—Matthew 10:28

I bless you, dear, beloved of God,
to stand strong,
Holding to the truth of Jesus,
In the face of vitriolic opposition,
And personal risk.
I bless you with the fullness of the Holy Spirit,
His overwhelming peace,
As He gives you words to speak,
And I bless you with the joy,
Of receiving Jesus's pleasure, commendation, and
honor
As you honor Him.

# Chapter 18

# Jesus Stood

*He is no fool who gives what he cannot keep
to gain that which he cannot lose.*

—Jim Elliot[42]

Stephen stood silently, bracing against the lies hurled at him. How ironic that his accusers, from the Synagogue of the Freedmen, descendants of Jewish slaves of Rome freed by Emperor Pompey, these very sons of freedom, had now seized and brought him captive before the Jerusalem Council.

A shout declared, "He speaks against Moses."

Then another, "And blasphemes our God!"

As a follower of The Way, Stephen was no stranger to personal attacks. But to be wrongly charged with blasphemy against the God he loved and served, and the prophet Moses whom he revered, pierced his normally thick skin like arrows pierce a straw bale. But he did not fear. Ever since the apostles had honored him with his selection to serve, he knew this day might come. The promotion made him a target of the Jews.

Still, he considered even their attacks an honor. Since his appointment as a deacon, the Presence of the Holy Spirit on Stephen's life had deepened. Jesus had become more real, and his intimacy with his Lord and resulting joy increased daily. The God he had been serving all his life was now very personal.

There was something else as well. Along with a growing peace and contentment, he experienced a growing power and confidence. Not in himself. He had nothing to offer. A power emanating beyond him worked within. He knew its source. The very Holy Spirit of the living Christ. Jesus miraculously healed those for whom Stephen prayed. And he confounded those who disputed the reality of the resurrection as this same Holy Spirit gave him the words to speak.

The enraged Freedmen had assembled an unlikely coalition of Cyrenians, Alexandrians, and even some from Cilicia and Asia. The frenzied mob seized him and brought him before the ruling council using false witnesses they had bribed to make their case. The heated atmosphere suddenly cooled in silence as his accusers completed their denunciation. Though their attacks ceased, the faces of Stephen's accusers turned toward the high priest, revealing a mixture of frozen outrage and hopeful anticipation of a sentence of condemnation.

"Are these things so?" the high priest asked Stephen as the attention of the throng turned back toward him.

It appeared again. Stephen felt the power. A pervading sense of calm radiated from his face as the calm waters of a shallow lake shimmer, reflecting the morning sun. In fact, if Stephen could have seen his visage, he would have been struck by an intense glow that those in the crowd would later say resembled that of an angel.

Then the words came. Not words of retaliation at the wrongful accusations. Not even words of defense as one might use to systematically pick apart and expose the failed logic of an opposing argument. The words passionately communicated a message welling up from deep inside. It was a message Stephen could no more contain than the effervescence from rapidly fermenting wine and expressed from a heart supernaturally filled with a great love for the hearers. Stephen began.

"Brothers and fathers, hear me." The message burst forth in full fragrance, the sweet wine of God's dealings with Israel whom He loved. How God longed to reveal Himself to Israel as He had revealed Himself to Abraham in Mesopotamia and to Moses in the burning bush. A message of God's purpose of honor for Israel, to worship Him and to bear the light of His Presence to the nations. And the message recounted how God had demonstrated His mighty power, delivering Israel from Egyptian slavery.

The sweetness of the wine turned sour as the message continued. Israel had not only rebelled against God's gracious invitation but had persecuted the anointed prophets of God's message. Those who falsely accused Stephen of speaking against Moses were themselves the actual blasphemers, rejecting and murdering the very One about whom Moses prophesied. An increasing boldness flooded Stephen as he felt the very heartache of God.

He continued, "This is the Moses who said to the Israelites, 'God will raise up for you a prophet like me from your brothers.'"

Stephen became more aware of how this would end. What their ancestors had done, they just did, and would continue to do as well. His fate would be that of God's anointed messengers who came before. Stephen gestured, struck by the steadiness of his hands and the slow, deep nature of his breath. Tears wetted his face with a mixture of love, grief, and holy anger he struggled to reconcile.

"You stubborn people! You are heathen at heart and deaf to the truth," he said. "Must you forever resist the Holy Spirit? That's what your ancestors did, and so do you! Name one prophet your ancestors didn't persecute! They even killed the ones who predicted the coming of the Righteous One—the Messiah whom you betrayed and murdered. You deliberately disobeyed God's law, even though you received it from the hands of angels."

It was done. The message delivered. The response didn't matter. Stephen could feel their rage as the only sound the stunned crowd could make was the low growl of hundreds of teeth grinding. He turned his face to the sky. As much as he had experienced the Holy Spirit, it was never like this. What he saw next overwhelmed him as one can only be when he beholds the glory of God. "Look," Stephen marveled. "I see the heavens opened and the Son of Man standing at God's right hand."

The mob understandably found their voice. They rushed at Stephen with frenzied screams, dragging him out of the city. Despite their fury, they would not act on such heinous intentions in the temple courts, not even within the city walls.

Stephen barely felt the stones as they pummeled his body. The glory of God transfixed him. Jesus still stood, His empty throne behind Him as one might stand to honor royalty suddenly entering a room. This was beyond Stephen's comprehension. He should be the one honoring Jesus. Stephen gazed at Him. "Lord Jesus, receive my spirit!" Then he fell to his knees. Stephen uttered his final words as he cried out, "Lord, do not hold this sin against them." And then it was over.[ao]

---

[ao] Stephen's story is taken from the Holy Bible, Acts chapters 6 and 7. Stephen's dialogue is taken directly from this source, although paraphrased in places using both ESV and NLT translations.

## Jesus Commends a Faith-Fueled, Spirit-Filled Boldness

Stephen's boldness is distinguished from that of Thalia, the Canaanite woman who approached Jesus with a desperation-fueled, humble boldness. Stephen's was a Spirit-filled boldness, fueled by faith in Jesus, enabling him to courageously proclaim Him in the presence of personal peril. Jesus commends those who remain faithful to Him, speaking truth about Him to others, unafraid of their response. He honors those who lay everything on the line, who hold nothing back, even at great personal risk, in their passion for His Kingdom and in their acknowledgement of Him. Hear the words He spoke to His disciples in Matthew 10:28–32, as they prepared for their first solo mission:

> And do not fear those who kill the body but cannot kill the soul. Rather fear him who can destroy both soul and body in hell. Are not two sparrows sold for a penny? And not one of them will fall to the ground apart from your Father. But even the hairs of your head are all numbered. Fear not, therefore; you are of more value than many sparrows. So everyone who acknowledges me before men, I also will acknowledge before my Father who is in heaven.

What was the source of Stephen's boldness? He was chosen as a man to serve some of the Greek-speaking Jewish widows, freeing the apostles for the ministry of the Gospel message.[ap] During his selection, he was described as a man full of faith and

---

[ap] See Acts 6:1–4

of the Holy Spirit.[aq] Faith is the thread that runs through these stories. Without faith, it is impossible to please God. And faith expressed in trust releases the power of God. But it is the Holy Spirit who takes our spark of faith and sets it ablaze. It is the Holy Spirit who removes fear and gives great boldness even in the face of death.

Those who are full of the Holy Spirit become like Jesus. It is only the Holy Spirit who can supernaturally enable us to love and forgive our enemies like Him. Consider the description of Stephen's death.

## Jesus Commends Those Who Forgive Like He Does

"And as they were stoning Stephen, he called out, 'Lord Jesus, receive my spirit.' And falling to his knees he cried out with a loud voice, 'Lord, do not hold this sin against them.' And when he had said this, he fell asleep" (Acts 7:59–60).

Consider the similarities to Jesus's death recorded by Luke.

"And Jesus said, 'Father, forgive them, for they know not what they do'" (Luke 23:34a).

And...

"Then Jesus, calling out with a loud voice, said, 'Father, into your hands I commit my spirit!' And having said this he breathed his last" (Luke 23:46).

What did Stephen discover about Jesus that day? He already knew Him as the Messiah, the Son of God, and the fulfillment of all prophecy. But Jesus took him to the next and highest level, that of forgiving his persecutors as He did. Only the Holy Spirit enables us to love and forgive as Jesus. This is the acid test of the Spirit-filled life and the highest form of conformation to His

---

[aq] See Acts 6:5

likeness. And it is one that Jesus commended, rising from His throne to stand in Stephen's honor.

*        *        *

The phrase "tip of the spear" often refers to those who are the first to enter battle—elite warriors who exploit extreme lethality in enemy encounters. The movie *End of the Spear* stands in stark contrast, chronicling Jim Elliot, Nate Saint, and three other missionaries making first contact by aircraft with the Waodani people in remote Ecuador in 1956. After an initial peaceful encounter, the missionaries are speared and killed by Waodani warriors, led by Chief Mincayani. Hear the last words of Nate Saint, spoken in the Waodani language as he lay dying on the sandbar where they had landed:

"I am your sincere friend!"

Nate's death, and those of his colleagues, understandably hit his sister, Rachel, hard. Yet, after a brief time, God compelled her along with Jim Elliot's wife Elisabeth, to join the Waodani. They became family to them, leading many to Christ. Years later, Mincayani and Steve Saint, Nate's son, traveled to the sandbar where Nate died. Mincayani confessed to the murder, offering his spear and his life to Steve, an offering Steve refused to accept. "My father did not lose his life; he gave it."

Jim Elliot's diary revealed thoughts he had earlier recorded. "He is no fool who gives what he cannot keep to gain that which he cannot lose."[43]

## Jesus Commends and Redeems a Sacrifice like His

Great sacrifices accomplish God's great purposes. But it is only a sacrifice motivated by love that suffices. What appears tragic is not wasted by God. It is used to accomplish His purposes. And it is a sacrifice of demonstrable love that often softens hearts.

Consider Stephen's deep love for his people. God used the resulting persecution of the church to disperse Christ's followers to Antioch, becoming a launching pad for the Christian mission to the known world. I wonder how Stephen's death affected Saul. Though he approved and was emboldened to persecute Christ followers, might the way Stephen died have planted a seed of conscience later used by God in Saul's encounter with Christ and his conversion? Paul, or the apostle formerly known as Saul, would later describe himself as the foremost of all sinners, yet was used by God to author almost half of the New Testament.[ar]

Nate Saint's and Jim Elliot's sacrifice of love, and Rachel and Steve Saint's and Elisabeth Elliot's sacrifice of love and forgiveness, led to Christ transforming an entire people. The world might have considered the Waodanis insignificant, but they were of immense importance to God. All of these mirrored the greatest sacrifice of love: Jesus's offering of His life on the cross, redeeming humanity, paying our ransom so we would be called righteous—so we would be called children of God.

As we wrap up our exploration of what Jesus commends, we'll notice our focus has been shifting. We have been moving from those Jesus encountered during His ministry to those in leadership positions in the church. However, Jesus still does not commend for accomplishments but for faithful allegiance to Him and love-motivated sacrifice. We will also notice the bar has been raised. The cost for remaining true to Jesus has increased. That cost can be the life of the one commended.

---

[ar] "The saying is trustworthy and deserving of full acceptance, that Christ Jesus came into the world to save sinners, of whom I am the foremost" (I Timothy 1:15).

A call to martyrdom is a unique calling, not universal to all. But Jesus does call those who would follow Him to a life of total surrender, of self-denial. Peter had tried to shield Jesus from His mission of atoning sacrifice when Jesus predicted His death. Jesus countered, "If anyone would come after me, let him deny himself and take up his cross and follow me. For whoever would save his life will lose it, but whoever loses his life for my sake and the gospel's will save it" (Mark 8:34b–35).

It is this surrender to Jesus that brings Him great pleasure and His followers great joy. It is the lack of surrender, as exhibited by the rich, young ruler in our previous chapter, that results in sadness.

Of the seven churches Jesus addresses in the book of Revelation, only two receive a commendation with no rebuke: Smyrna and Philadelphia. Although Polycarp is not mentioned by name, he is the bishop of the church in Smyrna. He is our transition beyond the biblical record. Let's see what he discovered of Jesus on his final day. His story is last.

*I know your tribulation and your poverty (but you are rich). —Jesus*

—Revelation 2:9a

I bless you, dear conqueror, beloved of God,
In the midst of persecution,
With a boldness to overcome,
To receive a revelation of Jesus,
So strong,
That it reframes your situation,
Enabling you to see,

As God sees,
And commands your attention,
Overshadowing those who seek your compromise.
I bless you with the joy,
Of His Presence,
Which overshadows all you suffer,
And as you overcome,
To receive His crown of life.

# Chapter 19

## Overcomers in Suffering

*Blessed are those who are persecuted for righteousness'*
*sake, for theirs is the kingdom of heaven. —Jesus*

—Matthew 5:10

Polycarp had not sought this moment. But neither had he avoided it. Since his dream of three days past, he knew this day would come. The vision of a flaming pillow under his head had been quite vivid, and though he had previously fled his house at the approach of the sheriff's men, he did not run again.

They found him at suppertime. Polycarp greeted the officers, astonished as they had been at his calm demeanor and strength, especially for a man of eighty-six. He called for food and drink for them, stalling for an hour or two of uninterrupted prayer before they took him away. Polycarp noted the regret on their faces as they placed him on a donkey and led him into the city.

Now as he stood before the proconsul, his resolve strengthened. He recalled the letter he had received from his mentor, John, one of Christ's apostles. His had been one of the first of seven churches in Asia to receive John's emissary and a personal message from the risen Christ, a message as bishop he had read repeatedly to his congregation (later recorded in Revelation 2:8–11). He had it memorized.

> And to the angel of the church in Smyrna write: "The words of the first and the last, who died and came to life. I know your tribulation and your poverty (but you are rich) and the slander of those who say that they are Jews and are not, but are a synagogue of Satan. Do not fear what you are about to suffer. Behold, the devil is about to throw some of you into prison, that you may be tested, and for ten days you will have tribulation. Be faithful unto death, and I will give you the crown of life. He who has an ear, let him hear what the Spirit says to the churches. The one who conquers will not be hurt by the second death.

*Be faithful unto death, and I will give you the crown of life.* Polycarp silently mouthed the words.

Then there was the voice as he entered the arena. "Be strong, Polycarp, and play the man!" Those brothers who were accompanying him heard it too. They searched to find who had spoken, but to no avail. A new voice interrupted Polycarp's thoughts.

"Are you Polycarp?" the proconsul demanded.

"I am," said Polycarp, surprised at his own composure.

"Have respect for your old age; swear by the fortune of Caesar. Repent, and say, 'Down with the Atheists!'"

Polycarp looked grimly at the pagan multitude in the stadium, each one holding high the certificate he had received for making the last annual incense offering to Caesar. He stretched out his hand toward them, saying, "Down with the Atheists!" His resonant voice left the stunned crowd silent. They turned their attention to the proconsul.

"Swear," pleaded the proconsul. "Reproach Christ, and I will set you free."

Polycarp stared at the proconsul, deflating him with a gaze that laid him waste. He staggered as if trying to defend a sword thrust as Polycarp's voice rang out. "Eighty-six years have I served Him," Polycarp declared, "and He has done me no wrong. How can I blaspheme my King and my Savior?"

"I have wild animals here," the proconsul said, recovering from his misstep. "I will throw you to them if you do not repent."

"Call them," said Polycarp. "It is unthinkable for me to repent from what is good to turn to what is evil. I will be glad though to be changed from evil to righteousness."

"If you despise the animals, I will have you burned," the proconsul retorted, seeking to rebuild his diminished authority in front of the crowd.

"You threaten me with fire that burns for an hour, and is then extinguished, but you know nothing of the fire of the coming judgment and eternal punishment, reserved for the ungodly. Why are you waiting? Bring on whatever you want."

The confrontation reached its climax, and the now enraged proconsul moved quickly as the willing crowd collected and arranged wood for the fire. Polycarp refused the nails that would have held him to the stake, choosing instead to have his hands bound behind him, a willing offering to his God. As the flames were lit, he prayed.

"O Lord God Almighty, the Father of your beloved and blessed Son, Jesus Christ, by whom we have received the knowledge of you, the God of angels, powers, and every creature, and of all the righteous who live before you, I give you thanks that you count me worthy to be numbered among your martyrs, sharing the cup of Christ and the resurrection to eternal life, both of soul and body, through the immortality of the Holy Spirit," Polycarp said. "May I be received this day as an acceptable sacrifice, as you, the true God, have predestined, revealed to me, and now fulfilled," he continued. "I praise you for all these things, I bless you and glorify you, along with the everlasting Jesus Christ, your beloved Son. To you, with Him, through the Holy Ghost, be glory both now and forever. Amen."

The battle was won. What happened next is best described by those who witnessed, recorded, and distributed a chronicle of these events:

> Then the fire was lit, and the flame blazed furiously. We who were privileged to witness it saw a great miracle, and this is why we have been preserved, to tell the story.
>
> The fire shaped itself into the form of an arch, like the sail of a ship when filled with the wind, and formed a circle around the body of the martyr. Inside it, he looked not like flesh that is burnt, but like bread that is baked, or gold and silver glowing in a furnace. And we smelt a sweet scent, like frankincense or some such precious spices.
>
> Eventually, when those wicked men saw that his body could not be consumed by the fire, they commanded an executioner to pierce him with a dagger. When he did this [a dove flew out and] [*this may well be a later interpolation or transcription error] such a great quantity of blood flowed that the fire was extinguished.

The crowd were amazed at the difference between the unbelievers and the elect—of whom the great Polycarp was surely one, having in our own times been an apostolic and prophetic teacher, and bishop of the church in Smyrna. For every word he spoke either has been or shall be accomplished.[as]

What did Polycarp discover that day about Jesus? He recognized Jesus as the eternally faithful One who he could trust with his life and his death. He also discovered how much God displays His Glory in those who surrender everything for the Name of Jesus. There is likely more Polycarp discovered about Jesus that day that is not chronicled. More we will never know this side of Heaven.

## Jesus Reveals Himself Deeply in Suffering

Polycarp received three revelations of Jesus during his last hours. The unrecorded revelation during his two hours of prayer prepared him for what followed. The reminder of the written revelation from John strengthened his resolve. The voice as he entered the stadium reassured and encouraged him. Polycarp remained firm in his faith and received the commendation and reward of the crown of life.[at]

The Father is always seeking to reveal Jesus to us. It is those who receive, embrace, and act on His revelation in faith that please Him most. We have looked previously at the pleasure Jesus received from Thalia, the Canaanite woman who called Him "Son

---

[as] This story and Polycarp's recorded words are based on Martyrdom of Polycarp (ca. 69–ca. 155).
[at] "Be faithful unto death, and I will give you the crown of life" (Revelation 2:10b).

of David." And Jesus took a special pleasure in Peter's recognition of Him as the Son of God. But now Jesus is doing more. He reveals Himself in a deep way to those who are suffering for His Name. And it is this deeper revelation that enables those who are suffering to overcome.

I sat next to another pilot on my airline flight returning home from my duty rotation and noticed his Bible open to the book of Revelation, the last book of the Bible.

"Have you figured it out?" I asked.

"It's about Jesus," he said, smiling.

A simple yet profoundly accurate answer. Revelation is the last book in the Bible for a reason. It is the climax of time and eternity outside of time. It is all about Jesus: His preeminence before, during, and after time; His risen glory; His role in the redemption of humanity and all of creation; His glorious victory over sin, death, and Satan; His splendor as the bridegroom welcoming His bride; the church; and His sovereignty as the ruler of nations! It is the most comprehensive revelation of Jesus throughout history and eternity. And in His revelation, Jesus commends those undergoing trials.

Jesus's revelation is also personal. He reveals Himself uniquely as if He is revealing the part of Himself that addresses the most significant need of the one commended. After revealing Himself to the Apostle John in chapter one, He reveals Himself to seven churches in the next two chapters. To each church in Revelation, He identifies Himself differently. He commends, rebukes, and makes a promise to those who conquer. Only two receive a commendation without rebuke: Smyrna, Polycarp's church, and Philadelphia. Although each church Jesus commends is enduring trials, it is Smyrna and Philadelphia who are experiencing the most intense persecution. However, Jesus also revealed Himself to two churches He did not commend, Sardis and Laodicea. These two churches had neither an accurate picture of themselves nor of Jesus. And there was one other characteristic differentiating them from the other five churches Jesus addressed. There is no mention of trials, suffering, or persecution.

Receiving a revelation of Jesus is the key to withstanding trials. We might even say the most accurate picture of Jesus, and of ourselves, is obtained in suffering. In Ephesians 1:16–23, Paul prayed for us to receive such a revelation:

> I do not cease to give thanks for you, remembering you in my prayers, that the God of our Lord Jesus Christ, the Father of glory, may give you the Spirit of wisdom and of revelation in the knowledge of him, having the eyes of your hearts enlightened, that you may know what is the hope to which he has called you, what are the riches of his glorious inheritance in the saints, and what is the immeasurable greatness of his power toward us who believe, according to the working of his great might that he worked in Christ when he raised him from the dead and seated him at his right hand in the heavenly places, far above all rule and authority and power and dominion, and above every name that is named, not only in this age but also in the one to come. And he put all things under his feet and gave him as head over all things to the church, which is his body, the fullness of him who fills all in all.

Paul's prayer bore fruit in the lives of many, including Polycarp, the bishop of Smyrna, who remained faithful in trial, and received a conqueror's commendation and reward.

## Jesus Empathizes with Those Who Suffer

We take comfort in knowing Jesus understands all our experiences, our feelings, cares, concerns, and fears, having undergone it all for our sakes. Listen to His words to Polycarp's church: "I know your tribulation and your poverty (but you are rich) and the slander of those who say that they are Jews and are not, but are a synagogue of Satan" (Revelation 2:9).

Jesus can empathize because He has perfect knowledge of all we encounter. Notice He also reframes, shows us a kingdom perspective on our situation. Though He is aware of their poverty, He declares them rich!

There is another reason Jesus can empathize with us. He has personally experienced all that we are experiencing and has overcome. The writer of Hebrews emphasizes this empathy: "For we do not have a high priest who is unable to sympathize with our weaknesses, but one who in every respect has been tempted as we are, yet without sin" (Hebrews 4:15).

## Jesus Affirms Those He Commends

Jesus sees the good in us, that which is pleasing to Him. Even amid rebuke, He begins and ends each letter to the church with an affirmation. It is not a general affirmation but a specific word about what pleases Him. Tragically, the two churches Jesus did not commend received a rebuke—and a severe warning. Sardis presented a false image, living off their reputation, but having no life. And Jesus described Laodicea, a self-satisfied and apathetic church, as wretched, pitiable, poor, blind, and naked. Yet even in these stern rebukes, Jesus affirms His love for those He disciplines and offers redemption.[au]

Do not fear a rebuke from Jesus. He never shames. Whenever He issues a rebuke, He often commends, puts His finger on what pleases Him, encourages, and promises a reward to those who persevere and overcome.

## Jesus Commends Those Who Suffer with Joy

"People are watching you." The statement, from an elder's wife at our church caught me off guard. I had just experienced a catastrophic job loss in 2003, and apparently people were curious as to how I would respond and what God would do. It was an emotional blow. Would I lose my faith? Lose my joy? I certainly experienced bouts of depression. However, God called me to forgive the person who let me go and to pray God would bless him and make him successful. As I did, my joy returned, and God provided another job for me soon thereafter. It was in the middle of all this that I was invited to become an elder at our church.

In fact, of the three times I have been invited to a leadership position in a church or ministry, each was during a time of suffering. One came after our second adoption attempt fell through,

---

[au] Jesus concludes His message to Sardis, "Yet you have still a few names in Sardis, people who have not soiled their garments, and they will walk with me in white, for they are worthy. The one who conquers will be clothed thus in white garments, and I will never blot his name out of the book of life. I will confess his name before my Father and before his angels. He who has an ear, let him hear what the Spirit says to the churches" (Revelation 3:4–6).

And to Laodicea, "Those whom I love, I reprove and discipline, so be zealous and repent. Behold, I stand at the door and knock. If anyone hears my voice and opens the door, I will come in to him and eat with him, and he with me. The one who conquers, I will grant him to sit with me on my throne, as I also conquered and sat down with my Father on his throne. He who has an ear, let him hear what the Spirit says to the churches" (Revelation 3:19–22).

and two came after job losses. During these trials, my picture of God, and how things are supposed to be, were shaken. But in my grappling with God and the questions I brought to Him, I received a clearer picture of Him, and of myself. My friend and prayer mentor, Pastor Fred Hartley of One Mission Church in Lilburn, Georgia, likes to say, "I never trust a leader who doesn't walk with a limp!" If wrestling with God in times of trouble, as did Jacob, qualifies for leadership and a commendation from Jesus, I joyfully accept!

Jesus commends those who respond to suffering with joy. It is not for those who seek suffering for suffering's sake. That would be masochism. It is not for those who seek to earn something for their suffering. That would be a corruption of faith and a mockery of the cross. It is for those who take the greatest delight in bringing Jesus joy, in seeing His Kingdom advance. It is a joy the apostles shared when punished for preaching Christ in the Temple.[av] A joy Paul and Silas evidenced as they prayed and sang hymns in prison.[aw] And it is a joy in trials of which James, the brother of Jesus, wrote that produces steadfastness and completeness.[ax] This is possible only to the extent that we have renounced our right to ourselves beforehand. Then what more can be done to us?

Jesus commends us as blessed when we suffer for His name with joy. He speaks in His Mountain Sermon, "Blessed are those who are persecuted for righteousness' sake, for theirs is the kingdom of heaven. Blessed are you when others revile you and persecute you and utter all kinds of evil against you falsely

---

[av] See Acts 5:41

[aw] See Acts 16:25

[ax] "Count it all joy, my brothers, when you meet trials of various kinds, for you know that the testing of your faith produces steadfastness. And let steadfastness have its full effect, that you may be perfect and complete, lacking in nothing" (James 1:2–4).

on my account. Rejoice and be glad, for your reward is great in heaven, for so they persecuted the prophets who were before you" (Matthew 5:10–12).

E. Stanley Jones, American Methodist Christian missionary and theologian, comments on this passage, saying, "It is not enough for one to be a peacemaker and be persecuted for his pains. He must know something of the meaning of the third, namely to 'rejoice and be exceeding glad' amid the persecuted peacemaking."[44]

Jones summarizes Jesus's remarks: "'Life is suffering—escape it,' says Buddhism. 'Life brings suffering—use it,' says Jesus."[45] Jesus receives great pleasure as we endure suffering for His sake with joy. And then He makes a promise, we will not experience the eternal judgment and separation from God of the second death.[ay]

## Jesus Commends Those Who Pay Attention and Overcome

Jesus commends those who go beyond just enduring suffering, even with joy. He commends those who pay attention to what He is doing with the suffering, how it is used for His glory and His Kingdom. Sometimes we will see it. Often, we will not. But it is our faith that trusts Jesus is accomplishing His highest purposes through our suffering that brings Him pleasure.

We highlighted how Jesus used the suffering of Stephen, the first Christian martyr, and Nate Saint in the previous chapter, neither aware of what their sacrifice would accomplish. And often, neither are we. But we use our spiritual senses,

---

[ay] "He who has an ear, let him hear what the Spirit says to the churches. The one who conquers will not be hurt by the second death" (Revelation 2:11).

awakened by the Holy Spirit, to perceive what He chooses to reveal. And as we do, our joy increases as we conquer and overcome.

What enabled Stephen, Polycarp, Jim Elliot, Nate Saint, and others to face suffering with joy? What is the secret to a joy that overshadows the trials we face? What is the key to a sustaining joy, even when approaching death? Let's look at the joy enabling Jesus to face the cross as we conclude.

> *Behold, I stand at the door and knock. If anyone hears my voice and opens the door, I will come in to him and eat with him, and he with me. —Jesus*
>
> —Revelation 3:20

I bless you, beloved of God,

With ears to hear His voice,

To hear His approval,

For what He sees in you,

which gives Him pleasure,

To hear His admonition,

For where you can grow,

And to respond to His invitation,

To dine with Him,

In intimate fellowship,

And to receive the joy,

Of His commendation and pleasure.

# Section 5

·· • ✦ • ··

# The Prize

# Chapter 20

# The Joy of His Commendation and Pleasure

*These things I have spoken to you, that my joy may be in you, and that your joy may be full. —Jesus*

—John 15:11

John the Baptist's fame drew groupies, or rather, disciples. One day they came to him with a complaint, no doubt concerned about his fading stardom. To paraphrase, "Hey, John, you know that guy you baptized? Well, he's baptizing people now, and everybody's flocking to him! What are you going to do about it?" I love John's response.

"The one who has the bride is the bridegroom. The friend of the bridegroom, who stands and hears him, rejoices greatly at the bridegroom's voice. Therefore this joy of mine is now complete" (John 3:29).

Can we comprehend that? John compares himself to the best man, who finds his greatest joy in the joy and honor of the bridegroom! And imagine the pleasure of the bridegroom in his best friend!

We find our greatest joy in pleasing Jesus, in receiving His commendation and approval, and knowing we bring Him joy. It is what we are created for and where we find our identity and sense of meaning.

## Jesus Invites Us into His Joy

I worked for a large company in the nineties as a pilot supporting their subsidiaries. Our parent company would give us each a turkey to enjoy every year at Christmas. However, a small band of the subsidiary companies would gather for a Christmas party as well. These were a group of people who interacted daily and enjoyed working together, and Kathy and I were invited to attend the party. As we were looking for a place to sit, the president of one of the subsidiaries invited us to join him and his wife at a small table. We were honored and gladly accepted! It was great fun to be asked to enter the joy that these colleagues experienced daily with each other.

Jesus does not just offer us joy. Like the host who invites us to a Christmas party rather than just sending fruitcake and a card, Jesus invites us to enter His joy, that which He tastes with His Father and the Holy Spirit. He summons us to join the party, to share in His pleasure in the context of relationship with Him.

Jesus tells a story of a master, preparing to depart on a long trip, who puts his servants in charge of his affairs, giving each a sum of money to invest. Upon his return, he commends those who had invested well, calling them "good and faithful." And then he gives an invitation. "Enter into the joy of your master" (Matthew 25:21).

There it is again. Jesus is inviting us into His joy!

Jesus shares an intimate meal with His disciples on the evening of His betrayal. Hear the words He speaks: "As the Father has loved me, so have I loved you. Abide in my love. If you keep my commandments, you will abide in my love, just as I have kept my Father's commandments and abide in his love. These things I have spoken to you, that my joy may be in you, and that your joy may be full" (John 15:9–11).

Jesus emphasizes the key to joy is abiding in Him in continuing relationship. Again, He is inviting His disciples to share in His joy, the very love He enjoys with His Father. How could Jesus talk about joy as He faced imminent crucifixion? It is this love of the Father and Jesus's love for Him that enabled Jesus to face the cross. This desire to present us blameless to the Father who then presents us back to His Son as His bride, stirred Jesus's passion. The writer of Hebrews encourages us to imitate Him. "Looking to Jesus, the founder and perfecter of our faith, who for the joy that was set before him endured the cross, despising the shame, and is seated at the right hand of the throne of God"(Hebrews 12:2).

## We Only See Reality in Relationship with Jesus

We come full circle here. Like Neo's blue pill/red pill choice, we only fully see reality in the joy of relationship with Jesus. We stand approved, adopted children of the Father, blameless in His sight, which stirs us to love Jesus and fuels a desire to bring Him joy and pleasure. As we have seen, Jesus receives joy not in great accomplishments, but in our simple expressions of faith, hope, and love.

Not only do we find our identity in relationship with Jesus, but we also see external reality as it is. Lauren Daigle's hit song "You Say" strikes a universal chord, having achieved major success in both Christian and crossover markets. The lyrics describe a struggle with condemning inner voices, and the reframing power of God's voice as the true source of affirmation and identity. And the faith expressed in believing what the Father says brings both Lauren and God great pleasure! If you are unfamiliar with this song, look it up. It will bless you.

Jesus addresses His churches in Revelation chapters two and three the same way. It is all about Jesus revealing Himself uniquely to each church as they need to see, commending, rebuking, and encouraging. He also reframes their reality. To the church in Smyrna that He commends, He reframes their perceived poverty as wealth. The churches in Sardis and Laodicea seek their identity from human recognition rather than in divine relationship, earning a rebuke. They are closed off from Jesus, content to live by reputation and human affirmation. They seek affirmation for accomplishments. They have been seduced by a religious spirit. But there is no joy in this. Jesus reframes their reality. They had taken Neo's blue pill, seeing themselves as alive, rich, prosperous, and self-sufficient. Jesus reveals their true state—lukewarm, wretched, pitiable, poor, blind, naked, and dead.

## Receive the Joy of Jesus's Commendation

What does Jesus affirm in His commendations to the churches in Revelation? Overwhelmingly, Jesus commends faithful, patient endurance among tribulation. And He affirms love for Him. His commendation to Thyatira encompasses love, faith, and patient endurance.[az] These are the same qualities of faith, hope, and love, evidenced in our stories of those whom Jesus commends.

Jesus also warns five of the seven churches to repent and reconsider. He doesn't want them to miss His joy and the rewards for those who conquer and overcome: a crown of life, authority over nations as co-regents, and a new name. And most of all, entering into the joy He shares in relationship with His Father. Jesus describes the Father's gracious invitation, and the tragedy

---

[az] "I know your works, your love and faith and service and patient endurance, and that your latter works exceed the first" (Revelation 2:19).

of missing it in His story of a great banquet recorded in Luke's Gospel (Luke 14:15b–24):

> A man once gave a great banquet and invited many. And at the time for the banquet, he sent his servant to say to those who had been invited, "Come, for everything is now ready." But they all alike began to make excuses. The first said to him, "I have bought a field, and I must go out and see it. Please have me excused." And another said, "I have bought five yoke of oxen, and I go to examine them. Please have me excused." And another said, "I have married a wife, and therefore I cannot come." So the servant came and reported these things to his master. Then the master of the house became angry and said to his servant, "Go out quickly to the streets and lanes of the city, and bring in the poor and crippled and blind and lame." And the servant said, "Sir, what you commanded has been done, and still there is room." And the master said to the servant, "Go out to the highways and hedges and compel people to come in, that my house may be filled. For I tell you, none of those men who were invited shall taste my banquet."

Can we hear the gracious invitation and intense desire of the Father to share His joy with those He invited? Can we feel His heartbroken offense at their refusal? Can we grasp the tragedy of what they had missed? The lukewarm Church in Laodicea resembles. They were apathetic, complacent, and oblivious to the joy of a relationship with Jesus. They may have not just lost the joy of their first love as the Church in Ephesus. They most likely never experienced it. This is a tepidness Jesus wanted to vomit, and which earned His greatest rebuke.

Astonishingly, however, Jesus did not write them off. He offered the red pill of His blood shed for their sin and ours, salve for their eyes so they could see reality. He offered white robes, the covering of His righteousness. He affirmed the love-motivated nature of His discipline and rebuke. And He extended the most intimate of all invitations, to dine with Him, to enjoy the fellowship of His banquet.[ba]

## Jesus Commends Those Who Hear His Voice

All throughout the stories we have considered, we find Jesus revealing Himself. And He is revealing Himself not to the self-righteous or to those of great accomplishments or abilities. He reveals Himself to the broken, humble, searching, desperate, and open—often those of questionable moral standing. He reveals Himself to the lowly, such as the Canaanite woman, and to the high, such as Zacchaeus. He is revealing Himself to you and me. And He commends and takes magnificent pleasure in those who see and respond.

To each of the churches in Revelation, He gives one common plea, "He who has an ear, let him hear what the Spirit says to the churches." What has He been saying to you as we have taken this journey together? How has He been revealing Himself? Whatever you have heard Him say, hear these words, spoken to His disciples, again. "These things I have spoken to you, that my joy may be in you, and that your joy may be full" (John 15:11).

---

[ba] "I counsel you to buy from me gold refined by fire, so that you may be rich, and white garments so that you may clothe yourself and the shame of your nakedness may not be seen, and salve to anoint your eyes, so that you may see. Those whom I love, I reprove and discipline, so be zealous and repent. Behold, I stand at the door and knock. If anyone hears my voice and opens the door, I will come in to him and eat with him, and he with me. The one who conquers, I will grant him to sit with me on my throne, as I also conquered and sat down with my Father on his throne. He who has an ear, let him hear what the Spirit says to the churches" (Revelation 3:18–22).

He speaks these words to us as well. Do you desire to experience the same joy in Jesus's commendation as those whose stories we have viewed? Would you join me in responding to Jesus's invitation to relationship, to enter His joy? All we must do is open the door, invite Him in. We don't have to tidy up first. We don't have to prepare a meal like Martha. He brings the banquet. All we need is to welcome Him. He takes much pleasure in our response to His invitation. He offers us great joy as we accept. Enjoy His feast!

Father, thank you for revealing yourself,
In your Son, Jesus Christ.
Thank you for the gift of the Holy Spirit,
Who reveals Jesus and transforms us to His likeness.
Forgive me for seeking to justify myself by my actions.
When you have provided my complete forgiveness
and justification
Through the blood and cross of Christ.
Forgive me for the times I have sought my identity in
the approval of man,
Rather than finding my true identity in you.
Thank you for opening my eyes to see as you see,
My ears to hear your voice.
And thank you for the gracious invitation to your feast.
Jesus, I open the door,
I invite you in.
May you receive the highest joy and pleasure,
as I respond to your invitation.
Amen.

# Commended

# Small Group Study Guide

*I also tell you this: If two of you agree here on earth concerning anything you ask, my Father in heaven will do it for you. For where two or three gather together as my followers, I am there among them. —Jesus*

—Matthew 18:19–20 NLT

We are wired to be in relationship. We are not created to be alone. God's original intention for us still stands. It is to experience joy in fellowship with each other and with Him. The word translated "agree" in the passage above comes from the Greek word "sumphoneo." It literally means to sound together. As you may have already guessed, it is the word from which we derive the English word "symphony."

We create a beautiful harmony when we come together to share our stories, joy, and pain. Our joy increases as we share our joys in God's Presence with each other. And our pain diminishes as we bear each other's burdens as well. Insights deepen as we hear each other's perspectives. We support and encourage each other as we share how we are applying what we are hearing from God, and what we are learning to our lives. This small group study is designed to aid in this purpose.

A series of group questions guide each session. The first is designed to help participants get to know each other better and connect. The remaining suggested questions delve into the material presented in the book. Although Scripture verses are not listed with the study questions, referring back to the verses quoted in the chapter you are considering will help you answer the questions. You may choose to combine sessions to fit the time frame you are committing to. Feel free to omit any questions if needed and focus on those most pertinent to the group's needs.

You may want to begin each session with a song. Anyone may bring a song they feel moved to share, a song that has touched them. Someone may also want to open with a short prayer, welcoming God and asking Him to reveal Himself. A time at the end allowing each who wishes to offer a short thanksgiving to God or anything they would like to say to God in prayer adds to the intimacy with Him and others.

One last observation regarding the opening verse in Matthew 18:9–20 is appropriate. Jesus shared this in the context of resolving conflict in the church. The goal of this study is to encounter God as a group in a safe, affirming, environment. We come together in the harmony of sumphoneo, encouraging and supporting each other free of criticism and advice-giving. Enjoy God's approval, affirmation, and pleasure, even on your worst days.

## *Session 1*

### Preface, Chapter 1—The Power of Commendation

Take time during this first session for participants to introduce themselves if they do not already know each other. Have someone offer a short opening prayer welcoming God and asking Him to reveal Himself. Reinforce the purpose of the group to discover what pleases God and results in His joy and ours and to do so in a safe environment free of criticism and advice-giving.

### Questions

1. Have you ever received bad directions from a GPS or another person? What happened?

2. What is your reaction to the author's question, "What if much of what we believe about pleasing God is remarkably wrong?"

3. Which of the statements about what drew you to this book (see Preface, pages ix and x) do you most identify with? What do you hope to get out of this study?

4. In what ways do you think David Bacon's relationship with his father impacted his life?

5. What was it about Billy Graham and the message he shared of God's love that changed everything for David Bacon?

6. What do you find to be missing, or less than satisfying, in your relationships with others?

7. Do you believe God is angry with you or disappointed in you? Why? Are you open to asking God to show you how He really feels about you?

Have someone open in prayer and thank God for your time together and His Presence among you. Ask Him to reveal how He really feels about you. Invite anyone to pray who wishes, and have someone close in prayer after everyone who wishes has prayed.

## Session 2

## Chapter 2—Consider the Source

Have someone offer a short opening prayer welcoming God and asking Him to reveal Himself. Allow anyone who has brought a song to share to offer it to the group. Reinforce the purpose of the group to discover what pleases God and results in His joy and ours and to do so in a safe environment free of criticism and advice-giving.

### Questions

1. What is the best costume you ever wore?

2. What do you think motivated Jacob to deceive his father?

3. Did Jacob's deception have its desired effect? Why or why not? What were the unintended consequences?

4. What labels have you accepted, either from others or self-labeling?

5. What sources of feedback do you tend to take seriously? What sources do you tend to ignore?

6. How did Jacob's wrestling match with God, and receiving His blessing, change things? Think about how this affected his circumstances, his relationship with others, his relationship with God, and his identity? How could this impact you?

7. How does God the Father's pleasure in Jesus affect you?

Have someone open in prayer and thank God for your time together and His Presence among you. Ask Him to reveal the pleasure He takes in His Son, Jesus. Invite anyone to pray who wishes, and have someone close in prayer after everyone who wishes has prayed.

# *Session 3*

## Chapter 3—It's Not What You Think

Have someone offer a short opening prayer welcoming God and asking Him to reveal Himself. Allow anyone who has brought a song to share to offer it to the group. Reinforce the purpose of the group to discover what pleases God and results in His joy and ours and to do so in a safe environment free of criticism and advice-giving.

## Questions

1. Tell about a time you tried to impress someone, and it backfired, or about a time you made an impression on someone without even realizing it or trying to.

2. How does Jesus's statement "Whoever has seen me has seen the Father" change your view of God?

3. What do you think most people, even those who identify as Christians, get wrong about God and what it takes to please Him? Why?

4. Why do you think believing in Jesus brings The Father so much pleasure?

5. Are you surprised Jesus rejected those who came to Him telling of the many great works they had done in His name? Why or why not?

6. What do you make of the surprise expressed by those Jesus commended for feeding Him, welcoming him, clothing Him, and visiting Him when sick or in prison and Jesus's response to their surprise?

7. How would you define "faith"?

As you close in prayer, thank Jesus for His Presence among you and ask Him to show you what you do that brings Him pleasure.

## *Session 4*

### Chapter 4—Faith: The Catalyst for Action

Have someone offer a short opening prayer welcoming God and asking Him to reveal Himself. Allow anyone who has brought a song to share to offer it to the group. Reinforce the purpose of the group to discover what pleases God and results in His joy and ours and to do so in a safe environment free of criticism and advice-giving.

### Questions

1. Tell about a time someone had faith in you. How did that make you feel?

2. Share your reaction to the author's description of faith at the beginning of Chapter 4.

3. Why is an invitation so important prior to exercising faith?

4. Where does faith come from? Why is this important?

5. Why do you think God gives "faith tests"?

6. What is the difference between faith and trust, and what does this mean for you?

7. Why do you think faith and trust are the essential factors in pleasing God?

As you close in prayer, thank the Father for the gift of faith. Ask Him to give you an invitation to take a step of faith, and tell Him that you trust Him with your deepest need. Be specific about that need if you are able.

## *Session 5*

### Chapter 5—A Great Faith, Chapter 6—A Bold Faith

Have someone offer a short opening prayer welcoming God and asking Him to reveal Himself. Allow anyone who has brought a song to share to offer it to the group. Reinforce the purpose of the group to discover what pleases God and results in His joy and ours and to do so in a safe environment free of criticism and advice-giving.

## Questions

1. Share about a time you received an affirmation, commendation, or act of kindness from someone you least expected. How did it make you feel?

2. How does recognizing Jesus's authority and our moral poverty aid in awakening faith?

3. Share about a time you boldly overasked? What happened?

4. Have you ever felt God was ignoring your requests? Did you give up? Why does Jesus encourage us to keep asking? Why did He not respond right away?

5. How are desperation and humility related? How does desperation help us exercise faith?

6. Why do you think Thalia's recognition of Jesus's Messiahship pleased Jesus? Why did she see it when the Jewish leaders did not?

7. How did Thalia's memory of past examples of God answering a foreigner's prayers help develop her faith? How does

remembering past examples of God's faithfulness in your life increase your faith?

8. How does Thalia's status as a foreigner give you hope?

As you close in prayer, declare your recognition of Jesus as the Messiah. Bring your most desperate needs before Him, even if you have asked before. This brings Him much pleasure.

## *Session 6*

### Chapter 7—A Seeking Faith

Have someone offer a short opening prayer welcoming God and asking Him to reveal Himself. Allow anyone who has brought a song to share to offer it to the group. Reinforce the purpose of the group to discover what pleases God and results in His joy and ours and to do so in a safe environment free of criticism and advice-giving.

### Questions

1. Have you ever met a celebrity? Did you have to push through to get close?

2. What opinion have you formed of Jesus? What more would you like to know?

3. How does the fact that Jesus is pursuing you affect you?

4. How has the Father been revealing Jesus to you?

5. Why do you think our seeking or pursuit of Jesus pleases Him?

6. What is repentance? What was it about Zacchaeus's encounter with Jesus that led him to repent?

7. Jesus did not ask Zacchaeus to repent. But Zacchaeus's encounter with Jesus resulted in repentance. Are you willing to allow Jesus to reveal Himself to you in a way that would lead to repentance?

As you close in prayer, tell Jesus you want a better view of Him. Thank Him for how He has revealed Himself to you. Express your response to that revelation.

## *Session* 7

## Chapter 8—A Great Confession of Faith

Have someone offer a short opening prayer welcoming God and asking Him to reveal Himself. Allow anyone who has brought a song to share to offer it to the group. Reinforce the purpose of the group to discover what pleases God and results in His joy and ours and to do so in a safe environment free of criticism and advice-giving.

## Questions

1. Tell about a time you asked a stupid question or about a time you refrained from answering a question for fear of appearing stupid.

2. What would your best friend say about you if someone asked your friend to describe you?

3. Tell about a time when you saw someone you knew in a new light, in a way you hadn't seen them previously. What happened to change your view?

4. How has your view of Jesus changed since beginning this study?

5. How do you understand the meaning of Jesus's death on the cross?

6. Nicodemus was confused about Jesus's comment "You must be born again." What is your understanding of this phrase? What does Jesus mean by "born of the Spirit"?

7. What caused Peter's blunder after recognizing Jesus's divinity? How does Jesus's response to Peter impact you. Does it give you hope?

As you close in prayer, thank the Father for revealing Jesus. Make a simple statement in prayer of how you view Him, e.g., "Jesus, you are..."

## Session 8

---

## Chapter 9—Hope: It Keeps Us Moving, Chapter 10—Her Last Resort

Have someone offer a short opening prayer welcoming God and asking Him to reveal Himself. Allow anyone who has brought a song to share to offer it to the group. Reinforce the purpose of the group to discover what pleases God and results in His joy and ours and to do so in a safe environment free of criticism and advice-giving.

## Questions

1. What do you most hope for?
2. How would you define hope? How is it different from optimism, or stubborn self-will?
3. How does hope build maturity? Where does it come from?
4. Eliana had given up any hope of being cured. What causes you to lose hope?
5. What reignited Eliana's hope and caused her to push through to reach Jesus?
6. How does unforgiveness block hope? How does forgiveness release it?
7. Jesus gave Eliana more than she was seeking. How does this impact your hope?

As you close in prayer, thank Jesus for the forgiveness He offers. Bring your most desperate situation before Him. Express trust in Him to bring resolution. Thank Him for His Presence even in the midst of your pain.

## *Session 9*

## Chapter 11—Justified by God,
## Chapter 12—None Is Greater

Have someone offer a short opening prayer welcoming God and asking Him to reveal Himself. Allow anyone who has brought a song to share to offer it to the group. Reinforce the purpose of the group to discover what pleases God and results in His joy and ours and to do so in a safe environment free of criticism and advice-giving.

## Questions

1. Have you ever felt uncomfortable in a religious setting? What was happening?

2. What was it about the Pharisee's prayer that repelled God?

3. What was it about Lavan's prayer that attracted God?

4. What is it about humility that pleases God?

5. What caused John the Baptist to lose hope or doubt? What did he do with it?

6. What renewed John's hope?

7. What pleased Jesus about John? What did He commend? Describe as many as you can.

As you close in prayer, thank the Father for His mercy and forgiveness that does not depend on our righteousness. Thank Him for the gift of Jesus's righteousness, which He freely offers. Be honest with the Father as you bring any questions or doubts you may have to Him. Thank Him for welcoming your honest questions, and express your trust that He will answer.

# Session 10

## Chapter 13—The Last Request

Have someone offer a short opening prayer welcoming God and asking Him to reveal Himself. Allow anyone who has brought a song to share to offer it to the group. Reinforce the purpose of the group to discover what pleases God and results in His joy and ours and to do so in a safe environment free of criticism and advice-giving.

## Questions

1. Share about a bad day you have had.

2. What is your reaction when you experience consequences of your actions? Do you curse and retaliate as did Gestas, or do you experience deep regret and remorse as did Demas? How was this regret converted to repentance?

3. Do you believe, as did Demas, that even in the experience of your consequences, and with nothing to offer, that you can throw yourself on Jesus's mercy and He will welcome you and gift you with eternal life? Is this too good to be true?

4. How did the Old Testament prophecy of the Messiah impact Demas? How does it impact you?

5. What is your rection to the Stoner/Newman statistical study of Old Testament prophecy?

6. How did Jesus's forgiveness of His executioners affect Demas? How does it affect you?

7. How did the events surrounding Jesus's death impact the Centurion's view of Jesus? How do these events impact your view of Jesus? How does this give you hope?

As you close in prayer, declare your view of Jesus. Confess your need for forgiveness. Thank the Father for offering His Son, Jesus, as an atonement for your sin and for His mercy.

## Session 11

### Chapter 14—Love: The Commended Motivation

Have someone offer a short opening prayer welcoming God and asking Him to reveal Himself. Allow anyone who has brought a song to share to offer it to the group. Reinforce the purpose of the group to discover what pleases God and results in His joy and ours and to do so in a safe environment free of criticism and advice-giving.

## Questions

1. Who is the most loving person you have known? What is it about them that stands out?

2. What does it mean that God's essential nature is love? How do you reconcile that with God's judgement of sin?

3. How is our ability to love related to our knowing God?

4. How do you respond to Paul's teaching in 1 Corinthians 13 that great faith, knowledge, power, giving, and sacrifice without love means nothing? How does this relate to Jesus's statement, to those who boasted of great works in His name, to depart from Him because He never knew them?

5. How does love relate to what Jesus commands? What does love look like?

6. How does the fact that God loved us first (even while we were His enemies) impact our ability to love?

7. How does Paul's prayer that God would grant us the ability to comprehend His love that is beyond knowledge, and Brennan Manning's assertion that God's glory and love is too big for us, affect you?

Ask God to reveal His love to you using Paul's prayer in Ephesians 3:14–19 as you close.

# Session 12

## Chapter 15—All She Had,
## Chapter 16—A Lost Innocence Restored

Have someone offer a short opening prayer welcoming God and asking Him to reveal Himself. Allow anyone who has brought a song to share to offer it to the group. Reinforce the purpose of the group to discover what pleases God and results in His joy and ours and to do so in a safe environment free of criticism and advice-giving.

## Questions

1. Share about a time you gave something you seemingly couldn't afford to give. What motivated you? What happened as a result? Have you ever felt embarrassed by the small size of a gift you gave?

2. What motivated Miriam to give her last two coins? What did she expect in return? Why did this please Jesus and elicit His commendation?

3. What motivated Mary to approach Jesus, even in a Pharisee's house?

4. Notice the difference in the size of Miriam's gift and Mary's gift. Why do you think both were equally extravagant in Jesus's eyes. What prompted these gifts?

5. Both Miriam's and Mary's gifts were acts of worship. How did their expressions of worship differ? How were their expressions of worship similar?

6. Where do you feel most free to worship? Where do you feel restrained or self-conscious and why? How do you express yourself in worship?

7. Who do you identify with more, Miriam or Mary? Why?

As you close in prayer, take time to thank Jesus for what He has done for you. Express what you desire to offer Him. Try something new in your expression of worship regardless of how others in your group worship. You may raise your hands or stand, as the Holy Spirit leads.

# *Session 13*

## Chapter 17—The Better Part

Have someone offer a short opening prayer welcoming God and asking Him to reveal Himself. Allow anyone who has brought a song to share to offer it to the group. Reinforce the purpose of the group to discover what pleases God and results in His joy and ours and to do so in a safe environment free of criticism and advice-giving.

## Questions

1. Tell about a time you had last-minute guests. What was it like? Did you feel stressed?

2. Do you think religious activities can distance you from God? How have you experienced this? What are the signs this is happening?

3. Martha was seeking to minister to Jesus by serving Him. Her heart was in the right place, but what do you think she was missing?

4. How can seeking to please Jesus by successful activity lead to developing a critical spirit?

5. What was it about Jesus's response to Martha that softened her heart and led to a transformation?

6. Do you identify more with Mary or Martha?

7. What do you take from the verse "Now Jesus loved Martha and her sister and Lazarus" (John 11:5)? Can you personalize this? Do you believe God loves you at your worst just as much as at your best? Why or why not?

As you close in prayer, confess any critical attitude you have had toward those who do not seem to be doing enough. Thank the Father for loving you at your worst.

## Session 14

### Chapter 18—Jesus Stood,
### Chapter 19—Overcomers in Suffering

Offer a short opening prayer welcoming God and asking Him to reveal Himself. Share a song someone has brought. Reinforce the purpose of the group to discover what pleases God and results in His joy and ours and to do so in a safe environment.

## Questions

1. Tell about a time you were falsely accused.

2. What enabled Stephen to speak both compassionately and boldly to his accusers without fear of the outcome?

3. What do you make of how Stephen forgave his attackers and the similarity to Jesus's death?

4. God used and redeemed both Stephen's and Jim Elliot's deaths to further the reach of Christ's Kingdom. How has God used tragedy in your life for Christ's Kingdom? How does this help you experience joy in suffering?

5. How does receiving a greater revelation of Christ provide the key for withstanding trials?

6. Consider Jesus's revelation to the seven churches given to John the Apostle. What does it mean to you that Jesus understands what we are going through? What is the significance to you of Jesus commending five of these churches even when he needed to give a rebuke? What of the two that received no rebuke? Or the two who received no commendation?

7. Which church in Revelation do you identify with and why?

Close in prayer expressing trust in the Father and thanking Him for joy, even in difficulties.

# *Session 15*

## Chapter 20—The Joy of His Commendation and Pleasure

Offer a short opening prayer welcoming God and asking Him to reveal Himself. Share a song someone has brought. Reinforce the purpose of the group to discover what pleases God and results in His joy and ours and to do so in a safe environment.

## Questions

1. How do you celebrate Christmas? Do you send gifts, invite friends to parties, or both? Do you attend a Christmas worship service? Where do you experience the most joy?

2. What does it mean to you that God invites you into the joy of the fellowship He enjoys as Father, Son, and Holy Spirit?

3. We live in a distressing time where we are presented with many different "realities" by the media and politicians. What is it about the joy of relationship with Jesus that enables us to see true reality?

4. How has the Father reframed your perception of reality based on what He says about you and His love for you?

5. Has the Father ever revealed the less pleasant aspects of your life to which you were oblivious? Are you open to asking Him to do this, trusting He will offer affirmation as well?

6. What do you make of the fact that Jesus extends His most intimate invitation to the church in Laodicea, which received His strongest rebuke?

7. Would you like to respond to Jesus's intimate invitation to dine with Him, to experience full forgiveness and the joy of relationship with Him He offers as a free gift? Would you like to receive the Father's promise of the Holy Spirit?

Close your time in prayer by thanking the Father for His invitation into His joy. You may pray out loud or silently. You are welcome to paraphrase the prayer at the end of the last chapter using your own words. After the time of prayer, share with each other in the group what this time together has meant to you. You may even want to have a celebration party during this last session.

May the Father bless you with the fullness of His commendation, affirmation, experience of His approval, and the joy of His pleasure in you. Amen.

# Acknowledgments

We all need affirmation. That may be especially true for writers who labor alone, often wondering whether what they are creating is "good enough." Not in the sense of whether the work will receive great acclaim, but more so, is it worth reading? Will it make any difference? Will it impact people's lives?

One of my reviewers congratulated me for "birthing this baby." Well, obviously, we can't birth a baby on our own! It takes cooperation from two in an intimate relationship, not to mention doctors who bring their professional expertise, friends who know us well and come alongside us with baby supplies and meals, and others who tell us what a beautiful baby we have made, regardless of how funny-looking the baby may be!

More than our need for affirmation, however, is our need for affirming relationships. Those who know us well commend what they see in us but also speak truth and reality into our lives. I am blessed to have many of these connections, some old and some new. They have come alongside me to offer support, encouragement, and professional expertise throughout the gestation of this work, and their DNA permeates this baby. They are those who did not just comment on the writing but also shared how it impacted their lives. For these, I am deeply grateful and wish to acknowledge their contributions.

First is my bride and joy of forty-nine years and alpha reader, Kathy. You had the first shot at me every step of the way. Your love, patience, encouragement, and honest feedback made this journey possible. "Many women have done excellently, but you surpass them all!" (Proverbs 31:28). I love you deeply.

To my beta readers Jeannette Smith, Dave Chapman, and Dwight Woodward who were among the first to view this manuscript in its raw form. Your feedback and encouragement kept me going. To Rich Montgomery and Myra and Mark Foster who reviewed a more polished version. Thank you for sharing how this impacted you and for your offer to help get the word out.

To those who knowingly and unknowingly mentored me. Thank you, Jerry Jenkins, for your Nonfiction Blueprint cohort. You provided invaluable wisdom on determining your why; shared a structure for planning, outlining, storytelling, and self-editing; and made all this and more accessible to new authors. To Fred Hartley III and Alan Wright, pastors and authors whose writing styles inspired me. You invested valuable time in reviewing this work and giving encouragement and great feedback, enabling me to improve the offering. And for Alan who lent his name and talents to writing the foreword of an unknown author. I am forever grateful.

To my editors. Beth Rodgers, your initial editing was indeed pristine. You caught mistakes in attribution and historical references. Thank you for your thoroughness. For the team at Ballast Books. Savannah, my acquisitions editor, thank you for your time in reviewing not only the manuscript but also the feedback I received and making sense of it all. Tara and Lauren, my manuscript editors, thank you for your expertise in CMOS formatting and professional layout and for your patience with revisions. And Kayleigh, my production editor, thank you for your patience in managing this project and for putting up with all my changes in cover design to make sure we got it right.

To Loren Jones, my cover designer. You do awesome work! Your enthusiasm for this project, quick turnaround, and gracious offer of your professional services were invaluable contributions.

To my reviewers, Kent Weathersby, Ronn Oren, Rich Montgomery, Storly Michel, Carey Edgren, Samuel Duraiswamy, Don Collins, Brent Burdick, Jim Bevis, David Beaty, Stephen Banda, and Ben Banda. Thank you for investing your valuable time to read, comment on, and endorse this work. Your reviews as well as your affirming email comments have been encouraging. I revisit them often!

I have been blessed to walk alongside those who have radiated much joy in vocational service to God, even if only temporarily. Nonetheless, they have had a deep impact on me and this work. The consistently grace-oriented shepherd pastors God has given me have poured much into my life. There are too many to mention, but you know who you are. Thank you. To CSI Ministries and One Mission Society who allowed me to serve in prayer ministry, thank you for your grace toward me and the many opportunities to see God personally at work around the world. You have opened my eyes even more to Father's grace and glory. To the dear folks at Rugby Chapel who invited me to serve as their pastor. Your love, affirmation, and honest feedback helped shape me. Thank you for allowing me to share messages with you that became the foundation for this book. The three years went by too quickly.

And to Jesus, the Great Shepherd and Commender. Thank you for giving your life to reveal the Father's grace and love to me. May you receive much joy and pleasure from this narrative. May Father use these stories of those you commended to reveal more of Himself to many.

# Endnotes

1   November 16, 2022, by Arthur Brooks, *Atlantic*

2   Ibid.

3   Wright, Alan D. *The Power to Bless* (p. 169). Baker Publishing Group. Kindle Edition.

4   Manning, Brennan. *Ruthless Trust: The Ragamuffin's Path to God* (p. 13). HarperCollins. Kindle Edition.

5   March 1, 2018, by Anna Douglas, *Charlotte Observer* (TNS)

6   March 2, 2018, by Brian Blackwell, *Baptist Message* Staff Writer

7   Robert Zemeckis (Director and Producer), 2000, *Cast Away*, DreamWorks Pictures, 20th Century Studios, Image Movers, Playtone

8   https://www.brainyquote.com/authors/c-s-lewis-quotes

9   Hartley, Fred. *Just Say Father: An Invitation to Be Re-Parented by God* (p. 24). CLC Publications 2021.

10  Hartley, (p. 17).

11  Wright, Alan D. *The Power to Bless* (p. 15). Baker Publishing Group. Kindle Edition.

12  Piper, John. *The Pleasures of God* (p. 31). Multnomah Books, The Crown Publishing Group. Kindle Edition.

13  Willard, Dallas. *Life Without Lack* (p. 25). Thomas Nelson 2018

14  Manning, Brennan. *Ruthless Trust* (p. 72). HarperCollins. Kindle Edition.

15  Frost, Jack. *Experiencing the Father's Love* (p. 60). Destiny Image, Inc. Kindle Edition.

16  Henderson, Daniel. *Transforming Prayer* (p. 154). Bethany House Publishers 2011.

17  Ian Charleson as Eric Liddell - *Chariots of Fire* (1981) - IMDb

18  Hamilton, Duncan. *For the Glory* (p. 350). Penguin Publishing Group. Kindle Edition.

19  Hamilton, (p. 179).

20  https://www.spurgeon.org/resource-library/blog-entries/21-funniest-spurgeon-quotes/

21  Manning, Brennan. *Ruthless Trust* (p. 19). HarperCollins. Kindle Edition.

22  Manning, (p. 19).

23  Manning, (pp. 2–3).

24  Wright, Alan D. *The Power to Bless* (p. 142). Baker Publishing Group. Kindle Edition.

25  Cymbala, Jim. *Fresh Wind, Fresh Fire* (p. 18). Zondervan Publishing House 1997

26  Cymbala, (p. 19).

27 Hartley, Fred A. *Hearts on Fire: A Guide to Personal Revival* (p. 33). CLC Publications. Kindle Edition.

28 Cymbala, Jim. *Fresh Wind, Fresh Fire* (pp. 25, 26). Zondervan Publishing House 1997

29 Manning, Brennan. *Ruthless Trust* (p. 30). HarperCollins. Kindle Edition

30 John 3:3 ESV.

31 John 3:4 ESV.

32 Manning, Brennan. *Ruthless Trust* (p. 3). HarperCollins. Kindle Edition.

33 Manning, (p. 86).

34 Chambers, Oswald. *My Utmost for His Highest*, Updated Edition (p. 253). Discovery House. Kindle Edition.

35 John 15:12 ESV.

36 Johnson, Bill. *Hosting the Presence: Unveiling Heaven's Agenda* (p. 124). Destiny Image. Kindle Edition.

37 Kasper, Walter. *Jesus the Christ* (p. 86). New York: Paulist Press 1977

38 Manning, Brennan. *Ruthless Trust* (pp. 101–102). Harper-Collins. Kindle Edition.

39 Dallas Jenkins (Director), Chad Gundersen; Justin Tolley (Producers), 2017, *The Chosen*, Loaves & Fishes Productions; Angel Studios; Out of Order Studios

40 Johnson, Bill. *Hosting the Presence* (pp. 133–134). Destiny Image. Kindle Edition.

41 Frost, Jack. *Experiencing the Father's Love* (pp. 80–82). Destiny Image. Kindle Edition.

42 Jim Elliot, https://www.brainyquote.com/authors/jim-elliot-quotes

43 Jim Elliot, https://www.brainyquote.com/authors/jim-elliot-quotes

44 Jones, E. Stanley. *The Christ of the Mount: A Working Philosophy of Life* (p. 77). The E. Stanley Jones Foundation. Kindle Edition.

45 Jones, (p. 78).

# Bibliography

Blackwell, B. (2018, March 2). "Billy Graham Shaped Inmate's Heart Who Built His Casket." *The Message*.

Chambers, O. (1992). *My Utmost for His Highest*. Grand Rapids: Discovery House Publishers.

Cymbala, J. (1997). *Fresh Wind, Fresh Fire*. Grand Rapids: Zondervan.

Douglas, A. (2018, March 1). "Who Made Billy Graham's Casket?" *The Charlotte Observer*.

Frost, J. (2017). *Experiencing the Father's Love*. Shippensburg: Destiny Image.

Hamilton, D. (2016). *For the Glory*. New York: Penguin Publishing Group.

Henderson, D. (2011). *Transforming Prayer: How Everything Changes When You Seek God's Face*. Minneapolis: Bethany House Publishers.

Hartley, Fred A. (2021). *Hearts on Fire: A Guide to Personal Revival*. Fort Washington: CLC Publications. Kindle Edition.

Hartley III, F. (2021). *Just Say Father: An Invitation to Be Re-Parented by God*. Atlanta: CLC Publications.

Johnson, B. (2012). *Hosting the Presence:Unveiling Heaven's Agenda.* Shippensburg: Destiny Image.

Jones, E. S. (2017). *The Christ of the Mount: A Working Philosophy of Life,* Kindle Edition. Potomac: E. Stanley Jones Foundation.

Kasper, W. (1977). *Jesus the Christ.* New York: Paulist Press.

Manning, B. (2000). *Ruthless Trust: The Ragamuffin's Path to God.* New Orleans: Harper Collins, Kindle Edition.

Mahaney, C.J. (2005). *Humility, True Greatness,* Colorado Springs: Multnomah Books

Piper, J. (2012). *The Pleasures of God.* Colorado Springs: Multnomah Books.

The Holy Bible, English Standard Version. (2001). Wheaton: Crossway.

The Holy Bible, New Living Translation. (1996, 2004, 2015) Carol Stream: Tyndale House

Willard, D. (2018). *Life Without Lack.* Nashville: Thomas Nelson.

Wright, Alan D. (2021). *The Power to Bless.* Grand Rapids: Baker Publishing Group. Kindle Edition.